Predictable Results in Unpredictable Times

Stephen R. COVEY Bob WHITMAN

with Breck England

Published by FranklinCovey Publishing, a division of Franklin-Covey Co.

ISBN 978-1-936111-00-8

Printed in the United States of America

Contents

Predictable Results in Unpredictable Times

*You are exposed to the improbable only if you let
it control you. You always control what you do.*
—Nassim Nicholas Taleb

Every summer a colorful crowd of cyclists race each other
in what is billed as the greatest human endurance test of all
time—the Tour de France. On the flat, sunny terrain, they
bunch up in a peloton, or platoon, some jockeying for the
front, some coasting along in the slipstream of a rider inches
ahead. But they mostly stay together. When the going is relatively easy, the peloton speeds along at a predictable pace.

Then comes the severe test of the mountains. Uncertain weather hits. Improbably, even in July the Alps can
produce freezing rain and sleet. By contrast, the desert-
like Mont Ventoux in the south of France is heatstroke
waiting to happen. As the cyclists climb thousands of
meters, the peloton strings out. Riders tire and drop
away. Teams fall inexorably behind.

It's in these extreme conditions that the great teams
take the lead.

At times, your team or your company or your organization will face extreme conditions, with steep terrain and dramatic changes in climate. No one can see beyond the next hill. Even in a turnaround, there's no likelihood of an easy ride—we've moved into a world where the measured risks of the past seem tame compared to what we face today. Future crises might be more severe than anything we've experienced. From here on, everyone agrees, we may be "in the mountains."

> The Tour is actually a team effort, and losing teams lack the disciplined execution of the winners.

That's when the great leaders will move into view.

Great leaders are different. They anchor themselves in principles that are certain and solid, even in an uncertain and fluid environment. They know the world is unpredictable. Still, they get predictable results.

How do they do it?

Before we go there, let's consider the reasons why so many competitors falter and drop out when they hit the mountains. It isn't usually a lack of strength or ability—most Tour de France participants are superbly conditioned or they wouldn't be there.

The Tour is actually a team effort, and losing teams lack the disciplined execution of the winners.[1] Winning team members must be able to trust each other without reserve to do their jobs precisely. They must be constantly focused, actively taking every opportunity to move the strategy forward. Otherwise, an accumulation of small mistakes will mean disaster.

Long experience with thousands of private and public entities around the globe has taught us that this lack of discipline makes all the difference "in the mountains." At FranklinCovey, we have studied the team disciplines of more than 300,000 people in 17,000 work units in 1,100 organizations. We have interviewed most of the people in 5,000 of these units. We combined interview results with financial, operating, and customer-loyalty data from a large number of "matched pair" organizations. This combined research has helped us understand the factors that truly differentiate top performers from lesser performers, the Lance Armstrongs from the also-rans.

Four Hazards of Unpredictable Times

Like the Tour de France cycling teams, companies trying to navigate in unpredictable times face four key hazards:

- Failure to execute
- Crisis of trust
- Loss of focus
- Pervasive fear

Failure to execute. You've thought through the crisis. You have your strategy. Now the question is, can your teams execute? Will they? Some people in your organization are getting it done. Some aren't and probably never will. Then there's the great middle—how much more could they contribute if they performed more like those who are getting it done?

Crisis of trust. Levels of trust drop in uncertain times. Securities markets plunge due to crises of confidence. People lose confidence in their own organizations. On an uncertain road full of pitfalls, everyone decelerates: it's not called a "slowdown" for nothing.

Loss of focus. You have fewer resources, fewer people, more confusion. People try to do two or three jobs at once. A person trying to do two jobs has half the focus of a person doing one job, and half the likelihood of doing either job well.

Pervasive fear. Economic recession causes psychological recession. People fear losing jobs, retirement savings, even their homes. It's "piling on." And it costs you. Just when you need people to focus and engage, they lose focus and disengage.

As you probably recognize, these four hazards occur together in times of turmoil. They reinforce each other. A crisis of trust stirs up fear. Fear and anxiety lead to a loss of focus. And a loss of focus puts strategy execution at risk. In such times, you simply can't afford to execute your strategy with anything less than precision.

To succeed "in the mountains," like the great cyclists, you must anticipate these hazards. You can dodge the hazards and win if you:

- Execute priorities with excellence.
- Move with the speed of trust.
- Achieve more with less.
- Reduce fear.

Execute priorities with excellence. The winning companies have "simple goals repeatedly revisited, together with clear targets and strong follow-through, including the measurement of results."[2] As with any great team, all team members know the goals and their roles in carrying them out. And they execute precisely.

Move with the speed of trust. Low trust slows everything down and raises costs. That's why the economy, your clients, and your cash flow slow down in times of turmoil. But when trust levels rise, everything speeds up and costs go down. The winning organizations are capable of quick action "with the agility to respond ahead of, or at least stay even with, rapid changes in the new economic environment."[3]

Achieve more with less. Of course, everyone is trying to do more with less, but the real question is "more of what?" Shouldn't it be more of what your key stakeholders truly value and less of what they don't want? The winning companies focus totally on value—they are not just cutting back, they are simplifying, reducing complexities that customers and employees don't value. Instead of having everyone do two or three jobs, they focus on doing the job that key stakeholders really want done.

Reduce fear. The root of psychological recession is the sense that people have no control over what happens to them. Winning organizations help people break through that hopelessness and focus on what they can impact. Much of the fear is caused by unclear direction, by a less-than-compelling purpose. Entrusted with a mission and strategy they can believe in, they channel their anxious energy into results.

If there's one thing that's certain about life, it's uncertainty. The great teams, like the great cyclists, perform consistently and with excellence, regardless of the conditions. This small book is about getting predictable results in good times and bad—whether you believe "this time is different" or not. The reason? You can rely on these four principles. They just don't change. And they will never let you down.

In this book, there's a chapter on each of these four essential principles, together with a plan to help you apply them.

One of the best ways to learn from this book is to teach its principles to someone else. It's a commonplace that the teacher learns far more than the student. So at the end of each chapter, you're invited to find someone—a co-worker, a friend, a family member—and teach him or her the insights you've gained from the chapter. You can follow the "Teach to Learn" guide provided or make up your own.

Execute Priorities
With Excellence

Winning on the flats is one thing—
winning in the mountains is another.
—Bob Whitman

In difficult times, winning performance depends on precise execution.

For the Tour de France, the mountains are the toughest challenge. This is the hardest part of the race where so much gets decided. Here the advantage goes not necessarily to the physically strongest team, but to the team that executes with the greatest precision.

Think about Lance Armstrong's famous U.S. Postal Service and Discovery Channel teams that won the Tour de France seven times. In the mountains,

> This is the hardest part of the race where so much gets decided.

the team became a "ruthlessly efficient machine." Day after day they consistently paced themselves at the front of the pack through the punishing Alps and Pyrenées.

According to one observer:

> George Hincapie, once a weak climber, now powered the peloton up the middle climbs of each stage. Floyd Landis would take the lead at the foot of the final mountain, setting a pace that splintered the field. Landis then handed off to Jose Azevedo, whose climbing pace was so fierce that only the top few riders in the world could keep up. By the time Armstrong rode to the front, he could focus on defeating the handful of rivals who remained.

Obviously, each team member knew his role and carried it out exactly.

By contrast, Jan Ullrich's team came in "eternally second" to Lance Armstrong's team. Ullrich was a brilliant cyclist who tended to lose energy on the uphill climb. His team behaved unpredictably, and in one mountain stage, one of his own teammates inadvertently defeated him.

The sevenfold achievement of Armstrong's Tour de France teams might never be surpassed. An observer called them "one of the greatest sporting teams of all time, and an example of what a brilliantly planned and flawlessly executing organization can achieve."[4]

Will the same be said of you and your team?

Maybe, but only if you do what the great teams do: make sure everyone buys in to and knows how to contribute to the goal and then "move the middle."

Does Everyone Know What to Do?

The mountains are the unpredictable part of the race.

The environment is changing like the weather. The landscape of your industry may be changing beyond recognition. Your resources may be stretched to the limit. What will you do now?

You're thinking, We've got our plan. Everybody knows what to do."

But you should be asking yourself, "Really? Does everyone understand and buy in to the goal? Does every team member know his or her role? Are they executing with precision?"

A great deal is riding on the answers to those questions.

One advantage of the mountains is that the goal gets simpler. On the flats where everyone can jostle for position, strategies for getting ahead can become pretty complex. On the uphill climb, the goal is plain: to stay alive and stay in front. But achieving that goal depends on each team member knowing exactly what to do.

For example, in a recession, everyone suddenly has the same straightforward goal: to preserve cash. Even profitability takes second place. Whether you're for-profit or non-profit, you've got to have cash or you close your doors.

So the CEO comes out with the cash-flow plan. It usually involves cost cutting here and efficiencies there. But what happens then? How many organizations meet the objectives? Is it because management doesn't realize

> One advantage of the mountains is that the goal gets simpler.

they have to preserve cash? Or is it something else? Does simply announcing a goal make it happen?

Today most business leaders are privately worried about execution. According to a report of the Conference Board, excellence in execution and consistent execution of strategy are now the top two concerns of CEOs.[5] Those issues didn't even make the list a few years ago.

And CEOs have reason to be concerned.

We have asked about 150,000 workers to name the top goals of their organizations. Only about 15 percent can tell us. Of that 15 percent, only 40 percent know what to do about the goals. About 9 percent feel a high level of commitment.[6]

Walk down the halls. For every 100 people you pass, 15 might know what the organization's top priority is. Take those 15 aside, and you'll find that only 6 of them know what their role is in achieving that priority. Six out of 100 are not enough to get you through the mountains.

Not true of your organization? Think again.

If you're the CEO, not even your closest associates may know your top priorities. In one major utility company, when challenged to list the company's 10 highest priorities, five top executives listed a combined total of 23, and only 2 priorities appeared on more than one list.[7]

The CEO simply can't assume that everyone is on board and understands the top priorities of the organization. (If you're not the CEO, you need to ask yourself if you know those top priorities.)

Suppose the "preserve cash" goal has been announced. Suppose every manager is aware of it. Does it follow that everybody knows what to do about it? Has everyone in the organization actively taken on the role of cash generator? Does everyone have a specific, well-defined job to do? Does everyone have goals in place for increasing revenue, cutting costs, and speeding up collections? Or are they leaving this all-important job to the sales office and the finance department?

If yours is like most other organizations, only a small percentage of the people are actively working on the strategy for getting through the mountains. The others don't understand the strategy, nor do they know how to carry it out, just when it's more crucial than ever.

In a crisis, narrowing the focus is critical. What if everyone in the organization had a laser focus on the one or two things that have to happen to get you through the crisis and emerge stronger?

> If yours is like most other organizations, only a small percentage of the people are actively working on the strategy for getting through the mountains.

The research shows that companies who win in tough times have "simple goals repeatedly revisited, together with clear targets and strong follow-through, including the measurement of results."[8]

If you lead by these same principles, you'll dramatically raise your chances of getting predictable results, even in a radically changing environment.

The great organizations, like great racing teams, have an execution system that ensures the predictability of results. Harvard Business School professors Robert Kaplan and David Norton make this point:

Most organizations have parts of a strategy management system, such as strategy planning, budgeting, HR planning, or performance reporting. But they function as silos, losing much of their potential value through lack of integration. Companies generally fail at implementing a strategy or managing operations because they lack an overreaching management system to integrate and align these two vital processes.[9]

In other words, you might have a good strategy, but without a good execution system, your strategy will fail.

So, what are the elements of a good execution system?

Our extensive research shows us that great performers do four things that lesser performers do not do:

1. **Focus on the top goals.** Great performers establish much higher levels of clarity and commitment among team members about desired outcomes.

2. **Make sure everyone knows the specific job to be done to achieve these goals.** Great performers involve team members in defining how those goals will be achieved.

3. **Keep score.** Great performers track measures that will lead to achievement of the goals and recognize and reward people for meeting those measures.

4. **Set up a regular cycle of follow-through.** Great performers conduct regular, frequent meetings where team members hold each other accountable for achieving the outcomes.

Let's look at each of these action steps in order:

1. **Focus on the top goals.**

On a December night in 1972, an Eastern Airlines jumbo jet from New York approached Miami in the darkness. Everything was in perfect order as the plane was about to land. Just then the captain noticed that the green land-

> In our turbulent times, you can't afford to take your eye off the key goal.

ing-gear indicator light wasn't on. The flight engineer went below and verified that the wheels were down, just as they should be. The cockpit crew continued to fiddle with the light bulb before deciding that it had burned out.

In those few minutes, no one noticed that the huge jet was rapidly losing altitude.

A frog hunter in the Everglades was first to the scene of the blazing crash. More than 100 people were dead and scores of injured survivors called for help in the black swamp.

What caused the crash?

Distracted by a burned-out light bulb, the crew had lost focus for just a few minutes on their most crucial goal: a safe landing.[10]

In our turbulent times, you can't afford to take your eye off the key goal. Organizations fail to execute their key goals when (1) there are too many goals, (2) there are no defined goals, or (3) people get distracted from the goals.

Too many goals. Our complex organizations produce plans containing thousands of goals that often have little impact and change too often. In tough times, you can't afford to dilute your focus on a host of goals that are anything less than decisive. The "Wildly Important Goals" are the ones you must achieve, or nothing else you achieve really matters very much. In really tough times, your one goal might be to just keep the doors open.

Think about it. If you have one goal, your chances of achieving it with excellence are high. If you have two substantive goals, you have just cut in half your chances of achieving them both with excellence. Three goals make things geometrically more chancy. And so forth.

Bain & Company's Orit Gadiesh says, "No company can be successful when it divides its resources among too many initiatives. Focusing on the right critical issues—no more than three to five, in most cases—is crucial to achieving success."[11] This is especially true "in the mountains."

> If your success depends on a critical goal, it's worth defining well.

No defined goals. Too many organizations have no goals to speak of—that is, no one can speak of them because no one really knows what they are. We've talked with thousands of managers and employees who can't say for sure what they are supposed to focus on. The goals, if they exist, are phrased as vague generalities: "save energy" or "get more revenue from online channels" or "become the leading provider of this or that." Fuzzy, poorly defined goals give people nothing to shoot for.

If your success depends on a critical goal, it's worth defining well. And it isn't defined well until the measure of success is clear. The best measure is always the answer to this question: "From X to Y by when?" Exactly how much electricity are we using now, and how much do we need to save by the end of the year? How much revenue are we making now from online channels, and how much more do we need to make this quarter? What does it mean to become the "leading provider"? Where are we now in relation to the leader? How big is the gap to be closed? And how much time do we have?

People get distracted from the goals. How often does the organization hold a big kickoff meeting to announce an important new goal, only to see the enthusiasm wane as the pressures of the day-to-day take over? How many corporate initiatives are underwater, buried by a high tide called the "day job"?

Suppose your crucial goal is to improve cash flow, and you ask everyone in the organization to make it their job. You must realize, of course, that you're asking them to do something in addition to the job they

> In bad times, the distractions are more severe than ever.

already do, which presumably keeps them pretty busy. Your chances of turning everyone into a cash manager are slim unless you regularly emphasize the goal, rethink their jobs, and minimize the distractions.

But in bad times, the distractions are more severe than ever. The tide becomes a tsunami. As people get laid off, the survivors have more to do. The distractions pile up to the sky as the economy grows rougher. Job insecurity, retirement worries, debt, and distrust make it harder to focus.

In Chapters 2–4 of this book, we deal more specifically with these distractions. For now, be aware that just when you most need the team's focus, they are less likely than ever to give it. Tough times are like that.

The first requirement of a good execution system is that everyone must know and buy in to the key goal(s). The leader's job starts with identifying the goal and communicating it, explaining it, making sure everyone understands it. There should be only one, two, or three well-defined goals—the fewer the better—to sharpen focus on what really matters.

It's the leader's job to eliminate or minimize distractions. Say no to less important priorities. "Shovel out" lesser commitments. Give team members the leeway to say no and to pare down their own cluttered to-do lists. Clear the way for them to achieve the key goals.

2. Make sure everyone knows the specific job to be done to achieve these goals.

A vast, sky-blue cargo ship slowly coasts from Copenhagen toward Bremerhaven. It seems as big as the sea itself. The *Eugen Maersk*, the world's greatest ocean freighter, is 400 meters long, with a propeller shaft a third again longer than a football field. New York's Empire State Building laid down alongside would come up 50 feet short. The cargo hold of the *Eugen Maersk* has enough space for 11,000 40-foot containers, called "cans" in the business.

In calm water, this complex ship is challenging enough to operate; but in the straits or storms, it requires total focus and precise execution. The sky gets dark, the winds whip up, the channel narrows. The crew, superbly prepared, moves as one person, each member sure of his or her role in securing the ship. The passage goes smoothly.

The *Eugen Maersk* is used to sailing in turbulent economic waters. One year, the ship bursts with cargo and even has to turn some loads away. The next year, the market collapses. Today, the ship is only half full. How to deal with this whipsaw of changing economic conditions?

In Copenhagen, the ship's owners are trying to do just that. Maersk is the biggest cargo shipper in the world. To navigate the economic storms, they have to operate at the lowest possible cost while maintaining excellent service. They've defined the goal and assigned specific measures to it.

Everybody at Maersk knows the cost-savings goal: that's why in the galley of the *Eugen Maersk*, diners use paper towels instead of napkins to keep costs down. And the leaders of Maersk want every team member to know his or her role in achieving that goal.[12]

Leaders decide what the goal is, but they don't decide how to achieve it; that's where the team comes in. Maersk trusts the people who do the job to figure out how to do it more efficiently and for less cost.

For example, Vice President Per Knudsen of the Maersk subsidiary Maersk Container Industri knows the goal, but the company leaves it up to him to decide how to achieve it. He belongs to an operation that constructs many of the giant containers carried by the *Eugen Maersk* and other ships, and he is constantly looking for ways to reduce costs.[13]

Per Knudsen did an Execution Quotient (xQ) Survey of his team.[14] The assessment helped him identify opportunities for achieving the firm's goal—and obstacles to achieving it that he wasn't aware of.

"After the first xQ assessment, we managed to do things we would not otherwise have done. For instance, we started work on a project specifically targeted at reducing the number of hours worked per unit produced. The results have not stayed away—the number of hours expended per container has decreased from about 42 to 34 hours." The new goal is to cut to 30 hours.[15]

The firm needed to reduce costs, but Per Knudsen and his team decided exactly how to achieve that goal in their operation.

Leaders who hand down goals must give teams the time and opportunity to learn how to achieve them. By definition, every new goal requires people to do things they've never done before. Nassim Taleb observes, "We have psychological and intellectual difficulties with trial and error, and with accepting that series of small failures are necessary."[16] It took a great deal of trial and error for the Maersk Container team to improve their processes and systems. But once they identified a few key measures to focus on, they cut production time by nearly 20 percent and gave a nice boost to profitability at Maersk.

Another firm announced its cost-savings goal and then went through an interesting exercise. Instead of dictating from the top how to save money, the leaders invited everyone to a mock "garage sale." They were to bring to the "sale" anything—any asset, process, or system—that they felt they could do without. Employees got to decide what to cut. Leaders knew that employees were best suited to make those decisions, and the firm slashed costs quickly and intelligently.

Lance Armstrong did not win the Tour de France seven times by himself. His team members—Hincapie, Landis, Azevedo, and others—executed precisely their roles in achieving the goal. The contribution of each team member counts, especially when you're in the mountains.

3. **Keep score.**

Picture the pilot of the *Eugen Maersk* guiding his great cargo ship through the straits. Rocks and narrow sea walls all around threaten the 400-meter length of the craft. He never takes his eyes off the screen that tells him within inches exactly where he is. His dashboard is full of indicators of all kinds—speed, fuel pressure, and temperature gauges—but right now his concentration on this one screen is total, his focus unbroken.

When you're "in the straits," you can't afford to pilot blind, nor can you afford to be distracted by a lot of less important flashing lights and buzzing horns. You've got to know exactly where you are on a few key measures. That's why any good execution system includes scorekeeping.

Smart leaders know that there are two kinds of measures to watch: lag measures and lead measures. Lag measures are the ones we usually think of because they tell us what just happened. Sales figures, expense reports, income statements—these are examples of lag measures. They are necessary, but you can't do much about them. They're history.

Lead measures, on the other hand, are predictive and influenceable. They tell you what is likely to happen. You can control them. For the Tour de France team, lead measures include "hours in the saddle," hill repeats, aerodynamics, and diet. Teams weigh every meal and count every calorie. One cyclist even rinses his cottage cheese to control his fat intake.

A weak leader focuses only on lag measures. He watches sales figures every week and calls the salespeople on the carpet for failing to meet quota. It doesn't occur to him to do something proactive, to help the team identify the lead measures that will produce better sales.

A strong leader focuses on lead measures. She helps the team isolate three or four key actions the team can control and that are most likely to bring the desired results (step 2 above). Then she tracks those actions consistently.

Effective leadership is a bit like a science experiment, involving a lot of trial and error. The team tries many approaches to influence the lag measures. For example, one construction supply company tracked the effect of email offers to wholesale customers. Two emails a week didn't seem to produce any effect at all. But when customers received three emails a week, sales jumped. Now the supply company keeps that number on the scoreboard to ensure that every wholesale customer gets three offers per week.

> A strong leader focuses on lead measures. She helps the team isolate three or four key actions the team can control and that are most likely to bring the desired results.

Elsewhere, the shoe department of a big retailer noticed that when customers tried on four pairs of shoes, they were more likely to buy two pairs instead of one. The department now keeps score of the number of pairs of shoes offered to each customer. Scorekeeping is time-consuming, but the lead measure is so important to the goal, that all the salespeople do it willingly. Furthermore, the staff is re-

> Accelerating performance means monitoring a few key metrics.

warded not just for meeting the lag measure (results), but also for meeting the lead measure (the action needed to achieve results).

Bain's Orit Gadiesh says this about scorekeeping:

> Accelerating performance means monitoring a few key metrics. These metrics go well beyond the deep pools of standard management accounting data—for the most part backward-looking and nonactionable…. Your blueprint determines the key measures that are required to track the success of the chosen initiatives; the company then drives the entire corporate language and rewards system around those metrics." [17]

In other words, instead of focusing only on backward-looking lag measures, focus on forward-looking lead measures.

Knowing the goal is not the same as knowing what to do to achieve it. It's not enough to announce the goal and then track the results; leaders must engage the team in figuring out the measures necessary to achieve it and then relentlessly track those measures.

4. Set up a regular cycle of follow-through.

On May 25, 2001, Erik Weihenmayer became the first blind man to stand on the summit of Mt. Everest. The ascent was grueling and dangerous, the success exhilarating. Unusually, nearly every member of Erik's climbing team made it to the top.

The goal was clear but unprecedented. The team around Erik had to face challenges no other climbers had ever faced before. Learning how to get through the treacherous Khumbu icefall at the base of the mountain required weeks of trial and error. In the process, everyone met in the team tent every night to eat and talk.

These tent meetings turned out to be crucial to achieving the goal. In each meeting, the team members would go over successes and failures of the day, turn them into lessons learned, and apply their new learning the next day. Then the cycle was repeated. Eventually, they cut the amount of time needed to cross the icefall from 13 hours to 2 hours; to summit successfully, this kind of speed was essential.[18]

Tent meetings were spare and short—after all, it was freezing and team members were exhausted. But that was an advantage. Everybody focused on solutions rather than simply reacting to the day's events or discussing them to death. They celebrated small achievements, made quick plans, and adjourned.

Achieving your team goals requires this same cycle of accountability. The mistake leaders often make is to announce a grand goal and then sit back in luxurious expectation that it will happen. If you never ask about the goal, your team members won't care about it. They have plenty to do already. If you don't revisit progress on the goal regularly and frequently, team members will conclude that you didn't mean it, and they will go do what they normally do.

At the beginning of the fiscal year, one firm held a grand convention of the entire workforce and handed out elaborate loose-leaf books containing the goal for the coming year. Leaders spoke eloquently about the significance of the goal to the future of the firm. The workers were asked to commit to carrying it out, and they readily agreed; after all, it was a good goal—a solid, strategically sound goal that made sense to everyone.

> Weeks went by, months went by. "How's it going?" the leaders asked each other, but no one could answer.

The first week after the convention, everyone talked enthusiastically about the goal. It would change everything, they said to each other. The second week, the talk died down somewhat. The third week, people were very busy and didn't think much about it. By the end of the first month, the goal was right off their mental radar.

Weeks went by, months went by. "How's it going?" the leaders asked each other, but no one could answer. At the end of the fiscal year, little had been done. The leaders were agitated, furious. How could the whole workforce of the company be so irresponsible? Hadn't they agreed to carry out the goal?

The problem? No regular, frequent "tent meetings." Leaders asked about progress on the goal only in quarterly performance reviews, if at all. Expecting everyone to perform automatically, they had put in place no cycle of accountability to help everyone focus on the goal. People are not automatons. When the leaders didn't follow through, everyone simply assumed that the goal was not that significant after all.

Great teams meet regularly and frequently—weekly at least, often daily—to review progress on their goals. These meetings are simple. Team members start by looking at the scoreboard to see where they are. They report on commitments made. They discuss lessons learned. They plan what to do next and make new commitments. These are not ordinary "staff meetings": the tent meetings focus entirely on moving forward the key measures of success. When team members can count on being asked repeatedly about progress, they know their leaders care and they want to contribute.

Again quoting Orit Gadiesh of Bain:

> A results-oriented mindset rests on developing a repeatable formula. This repeatability is the key to sustaining results…. It is a mindset that rewards an attitude that seeks solutions proactively rather than reacting to events…. It is the opposite of a passive, take-no-risk, "it happened to us" culture.

For example, in a division of the Nestlé company, "the workers meet after they finish their shift. They have a special room where they have all their performance data on the wall, and for fifteen to twenty minutes, they go through their own performance and they decide what they have to do in order to improve."[19]

In summary, to get to the point of excellent execution, a leader has four basic jobs to do:

1. Focus on the top goals.

2. Make sure everyone knows the specific job to be done to achieve these goals.

3. Keep score.

4. Set up a regular cycle of follow-through.

Are You "Moving the Middle"?

All right. Your strategy and goals are in place, the team knows what to do and what the score is, and you're following through. You've done everything you can to ensure a predictable result.

But then you look at performance across the organization and you inevitably see variations.

It's a fact of life. Some people and teams perform well, some don't perform well at all—and then there's the vast middle. The performance of any group of people anywhere always looks like this:

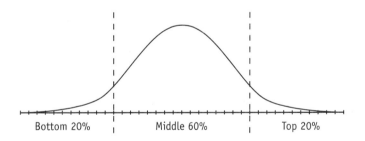

Bottom 20%   Middle 60%   Top 20%

See? There's that big bulge in the middle—these are people who could contribute much more if only they knew how. Now, think of the huge impact if that middle 60 percent performed more like the top 20 percent! What would it mean to your performance if the graph looked more like this?

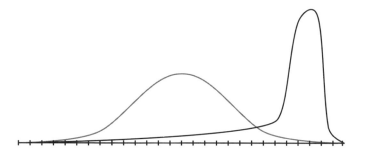

As a leader, your biggest opportunity might be to move the middle "right and tight" on the performance curve. You don't want to stay "left and loose": that means you get strung out in the mountain passes and lose your advantage.

What is the shape of your curve? Are you "left and loose" or "right and tight"?

In the Tour de France, the racers generally cluster in a group called the peloton, or platoon. This cluster behaves somewhat like a flock of birds flying through the air. The leading riders create a slipstream for those behind, making it easier for them to cycle.

Sometimes it's advantageous for a cyclist to drop back in the peloton where the wind resistance is lower. But a winning team doesn't want to stay there. Because the Tour is won by minutes and seconds, the winning team wants to lead the peloton as much as possible. Bringing a team member up even a meter or two from the middle can make a real cumulative difference in the mountains.

One of Lance Armstrong's team members, George Hincapie, was famous for his muscular sprinting ability. He could outrace anyone on short stretches, a valuable skill when needed. But in the mountains, Hincapie was relatively weaker, and the team needed a better all-round performance from him. Careful coaching made him a little leaner, a little better on the uphill climb. In the end, Hincapie took over leadership of the grueling middle slopes, staying only inches ahead of Armstrong to clear the path for his leader's final push.[20]

> But you should be asking yourself, "How can I get more people to do the things we already know how to do?"

For Armstrong's team, it wasn't necessary to come up with a big new strategy for the mountains. All they needed was to get each teammate to do the things they already knew had to be done.

The same is likely true for your team when you hit the mountains. You might be asking yourself, "What's the innovative strategy I need now?" And that's a good question.

But you should be asking yourself, "How can I get more people to do the things we already know how to do?"

Every organization has some team members, both frontline and management, who already perform with excellence. In our research, we have found that the biggest opportunity for performance improvement lies in moving the middle 60 percent closer to the performance levels achieved by that top 20 percent. Do some quick calculations, and you'll see the impact of moving that middle 60 percent just one third of the way toward the average performance of that top group.

Likewise, Watson-Wyatt's extensive surveys of business performance show that "the key to driving big productivity gains is increasing engagement among the vast middle group of employees—the core contributors who represent about 60 percent of the workforce."[21]

Do a little calculation of your own. Take the top 20 percent of the performers in your organization. What would it mean to your bottom line if the middle 60 percent performed at the level of those top 20 percent? Or even closed half of the gap?

To "move the middle"—to move your performance "righter and tighter"—you'll want to do two things:

1. **Identify islands of excellence.** Where in your organization are people already performing in exceptional ways? What can the "right and tight" ones teach the rest of the organization?

2. **Ask the team how to improve performance.** No one knows better than the team members what could be done better, faster, and at less cost.

Let's look at each of these action steps in order.

1. **Identify islands of excellence.**

In most cases, the greatest opportunity for improving performance lies in getting more people doing the things the top 20 percent already do. There are "islands of excellence" in any organization, "outliers" who perform significantly better than the average. Sometimes this is due to environmental factors—Store A in a rich neighborhood is bound to do better than Store B in a poor neighborhood. But even when you factor out the uncontrollable, some units just stand out. It's perfectly possible for disadvantaged Store B to be fulfilling its potential better than Store A in its rich neighborhood. In that case, we all have something to learn from Store B.

Look at your own organization. You know well enough that there are one or two salespeople who consistently rise to the top; one project team that always turns out high-quality work in record time; one school that outstrips the others in the district year after year.

Consider schools for a moment. The rewards for "moving the middle" in education are staggering. McKinsey & Company has calculated that if U.S. educational norms had historically matched those of nations such as Finland and South Korea, U.S. GDP in 2008 would have been between $1.3 trillion and $2.3 trillion higher.[22] Thomas Friedman of *The New York Times* observes:

> There are huge numbers of exciting education innovations in America today—from new modes of teacher compensation to charter schools to school districts scattered around the country that are showing real improvements based on better methods, better principals, and higher standards. The problem is that they are too scattered.[23]

The challenge is to turn those islands of excellence into new national norms.

This is your challenge as well: how to turn islands of excellence into the norm in your organization? Here are a few suggestions:

- Identify the islands. Visit them, study them, talk with them. Find out what they do differently. Communicate your findings.

- Raise the bar. Set performance goals that approach or match the average of the top 20 percent. Make those goals clear and use the execution system outlined above to achieve them.

- Tie incentives to meeting objective performance goals. Too many performance reviews end in a vague rating like "excellent" or "meets expectations," when everyone knows the rating is meaningless.

- Assign top performers to mentor others.

This is McKinsey's conclusion: "When large variations in performance exist among similar operations, relentless efforts to benchmark and implement what works can lift performance substantially."

Ironically, there are people and units in most organizations who are already superb performers. Your task as a leader is to move those who can and will change in the direction of those superb performers. You will find yourself building your organization around what works instead of worrying about what doesn't.

2. Ask the team how to improve performance.

The best people to ask about how to improve performance are the performers themselves. The lifeblood of your organization is in the middle. They handle most of the work, they touch the most customers, they know the terrain.

Bill Amelio, Lenovo's former CEO, observes, "We must ensure that our knowledge, our decision making, and our expertise in our organization are decentralised so that people that are very close to the ground can make things happen."[24]

If you want to improve the performance of a team, how hard is it to ask them about their successes? You might be surprised at the eagerness of the responses and the insights they bring. Ask them to tell their success stories instead of focusing so much on failures. A culture built around success stories is likely to create more exceptional performance.[25]

As you involve the team more and more in opportunities for improvement, you will not only move the middle in terms of performance, but also help them move out of the "middling mindset." There might be exceptions—and if so, you might rethink their employment—but few people really want to be mediocre. Most of your team members want to make a valued contribution—to find purpose in their work.

> Most of your team members want to make a valued contribution—to find purpose in their work.

To be mediocre is to fall far short of our potential. The startlingly gifted "hardware" we each have—a body, mind, heart, and spirit unique in the universe—is rarely called upon to do much more than fulfill a job description—the "software" handed to us by the organization. The vast untapped capabilities within us too often atrophy and waste away.[26]

Your task as a leader is to tap into the best the team has to offer. Great teams don't leave anything on the table. Your greatest legacy as a leader might just be that lean, powerful team defined by a Wildly Important Goal—the team that won the race when the race was hardest; the team that never let the mountain defeat them.

Strategy Execution Plan

These questions will help you pinpoint the actions you need to take to ensure excellent execution of your strategy. Take time with each question. Pose the questions to your boss, your team, and your peers in the organization.

1. Focus on the top goals.

- What are the most important one, two, or three goals of our organization—goals that absolutely must be achieved, or nothing else we achieve really matters very much?

- What one, two, or three goals does my team need to achieve in order to support the organization's top goals?

- For each goal, what are the lag measures that indicate success? (Remember to express them using this formula: From X to Y by When.)

2. Make sure everyone knows the specific job to be done to achieve the goals.

- For each goal, what one, two, or three actions do we need to take as a team to ensure achievement of the goal?

- How will we track the lead measures—that is, the measures of success on those actions?

3. Keep score.

- How will we display the lag and lead measures?

- Where, when, and how will we maintain the scoreboard?

4. Set up a regular cycle of follow-through.

- When and where will we hold our regular team meetings to account for progress on the goals?

"Moving the Middle" Plan

This procedure will help you improve the performance of the middle performers in your team or organization.

1. Set a goal for "moving the middle" to a "right and tight" position on the chart using the FROM X TO Y BY WHEN formula.

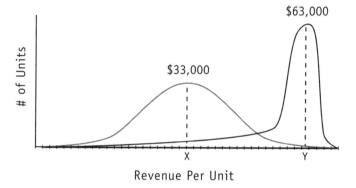

Sample Chart: In this organization, the key performance indicator is revenue per unit in thousands of dollars. The current average revenue per unit is $33,000 (X). The desired revenue per unit is $63,000 (Y), the average of the top 20 percent.

a. On the chart, plot the key performance indicators for each unit of your organization. This will give you a general distribution curve. The top of the curve is X, your current average. (Key performance indicators might be revenue for a sales group, speed of collections for a finance group, quality ratings for a customer-service group, and so forth.)

b. Plot the point to the right where you'd like the performance to be by a certain date. The top of that curve is Y, where your top performers already are.

c. Use the Strategy Execution Plan above to execute your goal.

    d. Each week, plot the progress on the graph. You will know if the middle is moving when X moves toward Y.

2. Identify the "islands of excellence" in your organization.

- Who are the "outliers" in meeting the key performance indicators?

- What action will you take to help median performers move toward the average of the outliers?

3. Ask the team how to improve performance.

- How, when, and where will you get input from team members on how to improve key performance indicators?

Teach to Learn

The best way to learn is to teach. It's a commonplace that the teacher learns far more than the student. If you really want to internalize the insights you've learned in this chapter, in the next day or so, find someone—a co-worker, a friend, a family member—and teach him or her those insights. Ask the provocative questions here or come up with your own.

- What generally makes the difference between the first and second teams in any competitive situation?

- Why do some teams and organizations perform so predictably well year after year, regardless of the conditions?

- Every organization works hard at developing a strategy. Why do so many good strategies fail?

- Which is more important—a good strategy, or good execution? Why?

- Is it better to have many goals, a few goals, or no goals at all? Why?

- It's one thing to have a goal—it's another to know how to achieve it. How do you decide what to do to achieve a goal?

- What's the difference between a lag measure and a lead measure? Which measure do you watch more closely if you want to achieve a goal? Why?

- Which is better—to let the team run with a goal without input from the leader, or to check progress regularly and frequently? Why?

- Which is likely to have more impact on your success—a grand new strategy, or doing better the things you already know how to do? Why?

- Why is there so much variation in performance across an organization? What would you do to reduce the variation and get better results?

- If you were a leader, what would you do to help people move beyond the mindset of doing just what's required toward a mindset of making a real contribution?

2

Move With the Speed of Trust

*"Widespread distrust in a society…imposes a kind of
tax on all forms of economic activity, a tax that high-trust
societies do not have to pay."*
—Francis Fukuyama, Economist

"In the mountains," trust makes all the difference.

Great Ormond Street Hospital in London has earned a reputation 150 years in the making at the forefront of children's services in all aspects of care, especially critical surgeries.

But at one point some years ago, seven infants died in quick succession following heart surgery. The surgical teams involved were devastated. Clearly, something was wrong somewhere. Not only was the crisis causing the public to lose confidence in them, they were also losing confidence in themselves.

A great deal of researching—and soul-searching—went into the investigation of these failures. Soon they learned that the most dangerous time in the surgical procedure wasn't in the operation or the intensive-care unit, but in the journey between the two. According to Dr. Martin

Elliott, "You have to disconnect the baby from a lot of kit, put it onto a trolley, move it down a corridor, reconnect to another bunch of kit, and transfer a lot of knowledge about the baby from one tired team to a new, fresh team."

After one discouraging day, the surgical team collapsed exhausted in the physicians' lounge. A Formula One auto race was on television when the surgeons noticed something remarkable on the screen. They became fascinated—not by the race itself, but by what was going on in the pit. When champion driver Michael Schumacher roared into the pit, the team that serviced the Ferrari racer went to work as if they were one person.

> The doctors leaned forward and stared at the screen, amazed at the speed, efficiency, and absolute precision of the pit crew.

Dr. Allan Goldman recalls, "A bunch of guys got themselves very organized, came in, changed the tires, filled up with fuel, exchanged a lot of information, and he set off again in 6.8 seconds." The doctors leaned forward and stared at the screen, amazed at the speed, efficiency, and absolute precision of the pit crew. "And that," says Dr. Goldman, "seemed to us to be remarkably similar to the process that we were going through." [27]

In the world of Formula One racing, the difference between winning and losing is measured in tenths, even hundredths, of a second. And although winning drivers usually get the glory, it's really a team effort that makes that microscopic difference.

The driver must stop periodically in a pit lane where a team of 20 or so highly trained people jack up the car, replace all four tires, fuel the tank, and make instant repairs. Obviously, they must do this as fast as possible—for every 10 seconds a car is in the pit stop, competing cars will gain about half a kilometer. The Ferrari team is one of the best in the world, and it was their high-speed precision that caught the attention of the doctors in London.

"I got in touch with them," Dr. Goldman says. "And we then went to Italy and showed them videos of our processes."

The Ferrari people were stunned at how chaotic it was—no one in charge, lots of conversation, lots of people in each other's way, unclear systems.

One mechanic recalls, "When we first saw the footage of the surgical team, I can remember thinking, 'Wow, they sure are disorganized.' We saw where people were standing, what they were doing when they were just waiting…. So it was no surprise to see them shuffle when the unexpected happened."

"Doctors, people like me," says Dr. Elliott, "are trained to help. So if you imagine that when the patient came back from the operating room to the ICU, it was a new challenge for everybody. We would all rush around the bed, getting in each other's way, all talking and trying to help.

"This is fundamentally opposed to the way in which the Formula One pit crew works. They know their job. Each one does. Silently they do it, and they get out of the way.

"They trust each other."

The surgery team learned quickly and soon introduced a system that defines carefully who does what and in what order. Every action is focused and productive; everyone has a contribution to make. "Now we know exactly where everything's going to be at any given time, while before it was very random," says an operating-room nurse.

> Today the Great Ormond Street Hospital cardiac team is one of the most trusted on the planet. In a crisis, you can trust your child's life to them without question.

Errors dropped by half. Patients thrived. "Seeing them get better and seeing the results improve dramatically—it's just magic," Dr. Elliott says with satisfaction.[28]

A Crisis of Trust

Today the Great Ormond Street Hospital cardiac team is one of the most trusted on the planet. In a crisis, you can trust your child's life to them without question.

But it wasn't always so. Their record was inconsistent. In the old days, you might have thought twice about trusting your child to them. You would have hesitated. You might have gone somewhere else.

It's not that the team members themselves could not be trusted. They were and are people of the highest moral character. But their systems and processes needed to be more trustworthy. There's much more to trust than just ethics.

Trust always affects two measurable outcomes: speed and cost. When trust goes down, speed goes down and costs go up. Distrust slows everything. Sales decelerate, customers grow cold, and team members get discouraged or drop out entirely. Distrust has hard costs. If you're distrusted, people will actively refuse to do business with you, your pipeline of revenue freezes, and in extreme cases you shut down.

Distrust has grown to global proportions. A crisis of confidence has overwhelmed the economy. The World Economic Forum cites a "crisis of trust and confidence" as the number-one challenge facing organizations in this decade. Business confidence is one of the top concerns of

> Because of implicit trust, a Formula One pit crew can do in seconds what it would take most people hours to do.

CEOs in the latest Conference Board Report of 2009—earlier in the decade, it didn't even show up.[29]

We have seen the downfall of major corporations over the trust issue. We have seen unprecedented loss of confidence in the financial markets. We have seen a global economy slow to the point where the flow of credit freezes completely.

But our purpose in this book is not to "point with alarm" at what you've already seen. It's to help you get predictable results in unpredictable times. And those organizations that get predictable results are the ones their stakeholders can count on to behave in trustworthy ways.

Just as distrust slows everything down and raises costs, the opposite is also true. Trust speeds everything up and lowers costs. You can do business in minutes on a handshake with a person you really trust. Because of implicit trust, a Formula One pit crew can do in seconds what it would take most people hours to do.

Trust Taxes and Trust Dividends

When things get intense, there are enormous parallels between a Formula One pit stop and your own team-work. You have to make complex decisions fast among team members doing different jobs under time pressure. And you've got to be absolutely trustworthy, or people quickly lose confidence in you.

An authority on the subject of trust, Stephen M. R. Covey, puts it this way in his book *The Speed of Trust*:

> The serious, practical impact of the economics of trust is that in many relationships, in many inter-actions, we are paying a hidden low-trust tax.... Mistrust doubles the cost of doing business.

> I also suggest that, just as the tax created by low trust is real, measurable, and extremely high, so the divi-dends of high trust are also real, quantifiable, and in-credibly high....When trust is high, the dividend you receive is like a performance multiplier, elevating and improving every dimension of your organization.[30]

Think about the hard economic dividends that flow to a high-trust team or organization. They sell more because their products and services are valued for con-sistent quality. Cash flow is excellent because delighted customers more willingly and promptly pay their bills. Costs are lower be-cause suppliers prefer to do business with them. Customers are loyal because they know they're going to be delighted with what they get.

> Mistrust doubles the cost of doing business.

Now think about the hidden taxes paid by a low-trust team or organization. Sales are slow for products or services of uneven quality. Cash flow is hampered by customer complaints, delays, and downright refusal to pay. Costs rise because suppliers lack confidence. Customers defect.

> The evidence shows that when the rest of the economy slows down, the companies that succeed actually get faster.

The evidence shows that when the economy slows down, the companies that succeed actually get faster. Breakthrough companies confront crises by actively and deliberately building trust, showing more transparency than ever before. Also, they act swiftly. They are able to leap hurdles that impede less trusted companies. During the market plunge of 2008, the stock of a group of such companies appreciated in value 24 percent![31]

Are You Paying Trust Taxes, or Earning Trust Dividends?

Now you're thinking, "Why are we talking about this? Of course my team is worthy of trust. They're great people and they know how to do their jobs."

But you should be asking yourself, "Is my team really trustworthy? Are we in fact trusted to do our job with excellence? Does everyone on the team know the job to be done? Is every system aligned precisely to doing that job?

"Are we paying Trust Taxes or earning Trust Dividends?"

Here are some examples of where you might be paying Trust Taxes or earning Trust Dividends:

	Tax	Dividend
Customer Retention	Customers defect when other choices are available.	Repeat business is a high percentage of your revenues.
Hiring	You have an unusually high employee churn rate.	People clamor to work for you and stay once they join.
Speed to Market	You experience long delays in providing services or getting products out the door.	Services are delivered quickly. Product development is smooth and timely and getting better all the time.
Meetings	There's a lot of positioning and politicking. People feel the need to "protect" themselves.	Meetings are open and transparent. People feel safe in expressing themselves.
Sales Cycle	Slow, protracted by hesitation, long negotiations, and carefully constructed legalism.	Streamlined and simple—buyers are open and confident with you.

The most trusted companies are the ones that have the competitive advantage in the marketplace. They earn big trust dividends. Is trust a competitive advantage for you?

A Tale of Two Teams

Now picture two work teams: a high-trust team and a low-trust team—both of them are going to make an important purchase. Watch the progress of the purchase order through these teams.

In the high-trust team, the meeting to decide on the purchase is quick and to the point because there is transparency and straight talk, no spinning or posturing. Because people feel free to share opinions, it's even hard to tell who's the boss.

Because others trust this team, the purchase order moves quickly through the organization. And in a high-trust organization, it requires only a couple of signatures and gets turned around in a day.

On the other hand, the low-trust team has a long meeting because straight talk doesn't happen. People leave the meeting unclear on the plan. Some get together "offline" for another meeting to talk about the first meeting, trying to figure out what was really decided. This spawns lots of email, private agendas, politicking, and badmouthing.

> Whatever your organization is like now, you can help create a "pit-crew mentality"

The result? Well, it takes a week instead of an hour to get the purchase order out. Then, because the team isn't trusted, the purchase order snakes its way through day after day of second-guessing at many levels. In this low-trust organization, five signatures are required, and the purchase order literally takes weeks to process.

Whatever your organization is like now, you can help create a "pit-crew mentality" of high-trust behavior, a team others can count on without question, a team everyone wants to belong to, a team with the "speed of trust."

Trust is not a soft issue at all—it's the hard, bottom-line issue of speed and cost. It can be measured and moved in the right direction.

It's possible to build trust fast and earn the resulting dividends. The solution is to carry out a deliberate campaign of trust building.

Rebuilding Trust

The Formula One team that inspired the doctors of Great Ormond Street Hospital was a team of unbelievable speed and precision. But it didn't used to be that way.

In the mid-1990s, Ferrari was a losing team. They had not won a Formula One title in nearly 20 years. Often criticized by the press for "notorious backstabbing," no one trusted anyone else on the team. At the same time, the team was known for its "unfounded optimism"; carrying the noble name Ferrari, they believed themselves the best in the world, despite their mediocre record and against all evidence: "The performance of the Ferrari pit crews was considered a running joke."

Then in 1996, everything changed. New CEO Luca di Montezemolo decided to revive the once-great Ferrari racing tradition. Some of the best people in the sport were lured to Ferrari to accomplish this miracle, and they made it happen.

What "turned this once-struggling team into the most successful in Formula One history"?[32]

The first thing they did was eliminate infighting and posturing by facing realities: a poor track record, outdated technology, and a culture of complacency. Soon they succeeded at building "a cohesive structure devoid of the polemics which were so rife."[33] Champion driver Michael Schumacher then took the team to six straight world titles, an unprecedented achievement.

Building trust requires high levels of both character and competence.

The Ferrari CEO knew he could only achieve pre-dictably good results with predictably capable people. In a crisis, you need your best performers around you and they need your trust. Montezemolo turned Fer-rari's auto sports division over to the best performers he could find, and trusted

> They held sessions after each race...to cut fractions of a second from the pit stop.

them to keep their commitment to get back on top of the racing world.

Ferrari also needed people with the character to face reality and tell the truth about it. The new team didn't flinch at the unpleasant realities—they were open about them. They admitted the problems and faced them squarely. Out of this transparency came a new attitude of respect for the truth and for each other.

The "cohesive structure" of the new team meant careful alignment of their systems and processes to the job to be done. In the pit, the crew worked tirelessly at eliminating not only major and expected sources of trouble, but also the little, unexpected problems that cu-mulatively slowed their performance. They held sessions after each race to log and resolve the smallest glitches in the continuous effort to cut fractions of a second from the pit stop.

Three Trust-Building Behaviors

Asked what companies should do in difficult times to build trust, Stephen M. R. Covey suggests three trust-building behaviors: (1) create transparency, (2) keep your commitments, and (3) extend trust to your team—exactly the behaviors that helped Ferrari climb out of a death spiral.

Create Transparency. "This is telling the truth in a way that people can verify and validate for themselves. Transparency is especially important if trust is already low, because people don't trust what they cannot see. So let them see it."[34]

There are too many hidden agendas, too much "spin" and positioning. Trust in what is said is at an all-time low. Howard Schultz, Starbucks' founder, makes this observation: "In the 1960s, if you introduced a new product, 90 percent of the people who viewed it for the first time believed in the corporate promise. Then 40 years later, if you performed the same exercise, less than 10 percent of the public believed it was true."[35]

> You can no longer hide a history of fudging or breaking promises.

Keep Your Commitments. Failing to keep a commitment depletes trust, and it depletes it fast. The common counterfeit to this behavior of making and keeping commitments is to overpromise and underdeliver—or to deliver activities, but not results. When you don't match the performance to the promise, there's a sense of disappointment and, ultimately, distrust.[36]

Remember, you're on Google, along with everyone else. Customers, investors, or prospective hires can research your track record in seconds. You can no longer hide a history of fudging or breaking promises. Be careful about the commitments you make, and keep the ones you do make.

Extend Trust. Ironically, one of the best ways to build trust is to extend it. And yet, many leaders withhold trust because they trust only themselves. The challenge here? Distrust tends to get reciprocated. When others don't trust you, you tend not to trust them back.[37]

Counterfeit trust takes the form of micromanagement. Great performers want to be trusted, and they will deliver. For those who don't—a crisis is a good time to invite them to "cross the bridge" or seek other opportunities elsewhere.

Case Study: Restoring Trust in a Crisis

When Anne Mulcahy became CEO of Xerox in 2001, the realities were brutal:

- Enormous debt ($17.1 billion).
- Declining sales and high materials costs.
- An embarrassing accounting scandal that was destroying trust in the financial markets.
- A fall in share price in one year from $64 to $4.

Hardly anyone trusted Xerox anymore. Customers and shareholders fled. Mulcahy was expected to act as a caretaker until the firm went into bankruptcy. The most anyone thought she could do was to preside over the orderly death of the struggling giant.

But Anne Mulcahy refused to let Xerox die and embarked on a deliberate campaign to rebuild trust.

Within a few weeks, she traveled 100,000 miles, holding meetings with Xerox clients and employees, giving straight and honest answers to questions about the company's future. As she explains, "If you schmooze and spin your communications, it comes back to bite you in your ability to establish credibility with people."[38] Gradually, she managed to increase trust levels by giving workers a reason to be hopeful and committed to the company.

Mulcahy made the tough calls:

- Restructured the company to cut annual expenses by $1.7 billion.

- Reduced debt by nearly $10 billion through shedding unprofitable businesses and activities.

- Paid a $10 million fine and opened the books on five years of Xerox's revenues to quiet the accounting scandal. (Authorities had charged Xerox with "spinning" financial results to meet Wall Street's expectations.)

- Put $1 billion into new product development based on careful analysis of customer needs.

Within two years, share price increased fivefold.

So how did Anne Mulcahy turn Xerox around? Essentially, she created transparency, kept her commitments, and extended trust to her worldwide team to restore the company.

Create Transparency. She was completely open about the realities, facing up to and righting wrongs. "I think transparency is important, and companies have to be into the role of clear and full disclosure," she says. "We live in a world today where transparency or credibility or authenticity—there are lots of words for it—but there has to be a sense of trust that needs to be apparent to the people you're asking to follow. And I think that's something that's become a lot more important recently than it was in the past."

Keep Your Commitments. She made certain key commitments for the future and focused on keeping them. "She had the guts to stick with her commitment to invest in R&D when it seemed everyone on the outside was calling for her to sacrifice it to save the company," says board member Bob Ulrich. "It turned out she and her team knew better."[39]

Recognizing that the old Xerox business model was broken, Mulcahy made the staggering commitment to transform Xerox fundamentally. "Gone are the stand-alone copiers. Graphics communications, digital imaging, new productivity services, and new hardware and software technologies represent the company's new offerings and sources of revenue."

Extend Trust. She extended trust instead of arrogating all decisions to herself and micromanaging her team. "If you run a big company, individuals don't really get anything accomplished. Teams get things accomplished. So the ability to build good teams, and have good teams that build good teams, is really the path to success in a big company."[40]

After six years at the helm, Mulcahy was named Chief Executive of the Year by *Chief Executive* magazine. Now that's a "Trust Dividend."

At a time when the whole world has been burned by extending too much trust to some important people and institutions, it might be tough to extend trust again. This is the hardest challenge of all. But the benefits of extending trust far outweigh the risks.

Stephen M. R. Covey tells of a Dutch insurance company that recently learned this lesson. The firm was struggling with the "Trust Taxes" of tremendous customer churn. "Their customers were turning over and leaving them at a rate that way outpaced the industry. They asked their customers why they were leaving. Basically, the answer came back: 'Because you don't trust us.'"

Because the company had been defrauded before, they had put in place a rigorous process of verification and validation for every claim. Whenever a claim came in, the message to the customer was: "You're a crook. Prove that you're not. Prove that your claim isn't fraudulent." The company was taking the approach that every customer was trying to cheat. The result? The claims process was laborious, cumbersome, bureaucratic, and time-consuming. So customers simply left.

The firm decided to reverse this approach and extend trust to the customer. Mutual trust increased. Speed increased. Claims that had taken weeks to process now took a few days, sometimes hours. Costs went down. To their surprise, the firm found that it was costing more to administer their cumbersome process than to reimburse claims.

> Whenever a claim came in, the message to the customer was: "You're a crook."

Just as they expected, customer loyalty increased. Customers liked it and stayed longer. But then a "Trust Dividend" came in that no one expected: the number of claims went down substantially. It turns out that many customers had been so resentful, they were submitting all kinds of petty nuisance claims. With "great glee and satisfaction," they had been clogging up the company's bureaucratic systems; it was their way of getting back at the insurer.[41]

A Trusted Character

These and other trust-building behaviors—such as demonstrating respect, listening, continuously improving your operations—are essential when you're facing a crisis of trust. But even more fundamental to your trustworthiness is

> The economic breakdown is about a breakdown in moral authority.

your own character. Your capabilities might even fail you from time to time, but good character never fails. There are times when you might not know what to do, but you will still know what is right.

No one leads without followers, and just as your team trusts your competence, they must also be able to trust your character—or they won't follow. It might take a while, but eventually, they will abandon you.

You're probably in your leadership position because of your skills, and your team will defer to your positional authority up to a point. They will not, however, trust you unless you also have moral authority. The economic breakdown is about a breakdown in moral authority.

Moral authority comes from two commitments: to act with unshakable integrity and honorable intent.

One of the most respected leaders in business is Bill George, former CEO of Medtronic. Under his guidance, the firm's value rose from $1.6 billion to $60 billion between 1989 and his retirement in 2001. About today's crisis of trust in leadership, he says:

I think we've had way too many leaders who are in it for themselves. They're more focused on charisma, style, and image than they are on character, substance, and integrity. We need leaders of genuine integrity who are committed to building the organization and will inspire others to step up and lead. There's no doubt that failed leadership is at the heart of the crisis on Wall Street.[42]

People simply will not trust leaders whose integrity is questionable or whose motives come down to "what's in it for me."

We all know about the sad spectacle of organizations that have been wiped out in a day because of a sudden failure of trust, such as the ironically named Integrity Bank of Atlanta, a "faith-based" bank whose founders poured millions into bad Florida real-estate loans and pocketed a good deal for themselves.[43]

INSEAD Professor Quy Nguyen Huy says, "What [leaders] need to focus on now is genuinely building trust through transparency and consistency between words and actions, which has been missing in the last several years, engendering much mistrust, contempt, and anger."[44]

Clearly, you want personally to be a model of integrity and good intent, and you want to lead a team known for the same qualities. For in addition to its intrinsic value, good character also pays off in hard economic terms—Trust Dividends. As Patricia Aburdene says in her book *Megatrends 2010*, "What we don't yet realize is that the moral high ground is actually very profitable."[45]

Companies that do well in tough times exhibit real character as well as strong capabilities. IBM and Procter & Gamble, for example, continued to report their usual respectable financial results, even during the slow years of 2008–2009. "Why are these companies faring okay today?" asks Harvard business professor Rosabeth Moss Kanter. A key reason is their "reemphasis on values and ethics…their feeling of obligation to leave a positive mark on the world. They do not stop feeling it just because the going suddenly got tough."[46]

> What we don't yet realize is that the moral high ground is actually very profitable.

A key difference between companies like these and the "Integrity Banks" of the world is trustworthy character.

A Deliberate Campaign of Trust Building

Our own research indicates that at least one in two work teams has serious trust issues. According to a joint FranklinCovey-HarrisInteractive survey, 35 percent of American workers agree that their teams struggle in major ways with bureaucratic rules and procedures, silos, slow approvals, misaligned structures, and complacent stakeholders. One in five workers suffers from very low or nonexistent trust levels: "Defensiveness, hidden agendas, political camps, excessive employee turnover, management-labor disputes, customer churn, dissatisfied stakeholders"—these are some of the symptoms.[47] Some 47 percent of work teams—nearly half—are paying exorbitant Trust Taxes.

If you recognize any of these symptoms, you'll want to start a deliberate campaign of trust building. The following Trust Action Plan will help you stop paying Trust Taxes and start reaping Trust Dividends.

Trust Action Plan

This planning tool will help you pinpoint the actions you need to take now to build trustworthiness.

Part 1: Where are you paying Trust Taxes that you could turn into Trust Dividends?

Rate your team's systems and processes to determine where you need improvement:

	Nonexistent	Weak	Mediocre	Good	Excellent	World-class
Decision making						
Financial processing (expenses, invoices, etc.)						
Internal communication						
Budgeting						
Performance management						
Employee orientation						
Training						
Strategic planning						
Customer feedback						
Marketing						
Meeting management						
Information systems						
Product development and innovation						

Part 2: Where can you realize the biggest impact?

Choose one, two, or three of the systems and processes above to work on and fill in the plan below.

System or Process	**Create Transparency.** Describe the current situation clearly and factually. Communicate it straightforwardly to the team. In what ways might you be paying Trust Taxes? What Trust Dividends could you earn by changing the situation?

Keep Commitments. Define your goal for improving the process or system. Commit to a time frame and keep the commitment.	**Extend Trust.** Identify the people who should be accountable for the commitment. Make your expectations clear and hold them accountable for the results.

Teach to Learn

The best way to learn is to teach. It's a commonplace that the teacher learns far more than the student. If you really want to internalize the insights you've learned in this chapter, in the next day or so, find someone—a co-worker, a friend, a family member—and teach him or her those insights. Ask the provocative questions here or come up with your own.

- In times of crisis, trust makes all the difference. Why is this so? What measurable difference does trust make?

- "Widespread distrust in a society...imposes a kind of tax on all forms of economic activity, a tax that high-trust societies do not have to pay." —Francis Fukuyama, Economist. Ask your partner what this quotation means. How is trust an economic issue?

- What "Trust Taxes" do we pay because of widespread distrust?

- What "Trust Dividends" come to people or organizations who are highly trusted?

- What happens to speed and costs in a low-trust situation? What examples can you think of?

- What happens to speed and costs in a high-trust situation? What examples can you think of?

- Why is trust a question of processes and systems, and not just moral qualities?

- Why is complete transparency so important to building trust? What is the opposite of transparency?

- Why does trust depend on keeping commitments? What happens if you fail to deliver on your commitments?

- Why is it important to trust others in order to be trusted?

- Why do you need both good capabilities and good character to be trusted?

3

Achieve More With Less

*We need to ask ourselves whether times like these
require getting the most things done, or a sharp focus on
getting the most important thing done.*
— Vineet Nayar, IT Executive

"In the mountains," it's not enough to do more with less—you need to do more of what matters.

Imagine what it takes to climb the highest peak on each of the seven continents, including Mt. Everest. Imagine what it's like when the temperature is far below freezing, the wind is trying to tear you off the mountain, and you're scrambling for a handhold on vertical ice.

Now try doing all of that blind.

Erik Weihenmayer has done it. The first blind man to reach the seven peaks, he knows perhaps more than anyone living what is required to succeed in extreme conditions. What do you really need to have with you when the going gets nearly impossible? Here's his advice:

> Talk about packing for a mountain, you're carrying your house on your back, and you can't carry

everything you want. So you pack light. As you get higher up the mountain and it gets harder, you have to become more strategic and focused and drop a lot of the extraneous stuff that weighs you down and becomes a distraction, all those obligations that you thought defined you. You have to strip yourself down and become more nimble so you can achieve the thing you really want. And when you're on the side of Mt. Vinson in Antarctica and it's 50 below, you might have to drop your pack altogether.[48]

Everyone knows that in a crisis, you have to do more with less. We all have to "pack light." But the important thing is to pack strategically. And the more challenging the times, the more "strategic and focused" we need to be.

You're probably thinking, "We are packing light. We've done our retrenching and hunkering down. We've kept our best people and we're moving forward."

No doubt. But here are some further questions: "What does 'more with less' really mean? Does it mean trying to do everything you did before, but with fewer people? You say you're doing more with less—but more of what?"

> The more challenging the times, the more "strategic and focused" we need to be.

A turn in the economy can hurt you, but your own decisions can hurt you even more. In a downturn, most organizations go right to work jettisoning people, turning assets into cash, shutting down capital projects. They roll up like armadillos and wait for the bad stuff to pass.

The organizations that succeed in the crisis do many of these same things, but more effectively. They differ in two significant ways:

1. Successful organizations tighten focus on building customer and employee loyalty.

2. Then they push the "reset" button to align the organization around those priorities.

Building Customer and Employee Loyalty

When you're trying to do more with less, the real question is "more of what?" Shouldn't it be more of what customers value and will pay for? Shouldn't it be more of what employees value and will stay for?

When Ann Mulcahy took over Xerox in 2001, the company was headed over a cliff. Share price, revenues, the reputation of the firm—all had plummeted. The first thing she did? Put through a phone call to the legendary investor Warren Buffett: "What do you think I should do?"

Buffett's advice: *"Focus on your customers, and lead your people as though their lives depended on your success."*

She took this advice seriously. Within four years, Xerox was once again profitable and out of core debt. Share price rose fivefold. Mulcahy attributes this remarkable turnaround to following Buffett's advice; it helped her "filter out

> When you're trying to do more with less, the real question is "more of what?"

the noise and focus on the two constituencies that matter most."

Above all, Mulcahy stressed the importance of focus on customer value: "Make customers the priority throughout the company by asking the question again and again: Would the customer pay for this?"[49] She emphasized maintaining customer loyalty while other key leaders grappled with the business issues. "We 'fenced off' and insured that our customer communications were flawless, that our customers didn't feel the impact of the crisis. It became everyone's responsibility. I think people 'got it.'"[50]

Mulcahy focused equally on her co-workers, "capitalizing on the loyalty of fellow Xerox employees." The average tenure of a Xerox employee was 15 years, so there was already a strong sense of identity with the company. To leverage this, in her first year, she traveled 100,000 miles to visit the firm's various locations and meet face to face with everyone, appealing directly for their help.[51] She recalls:

> Our employees were extraordinary. They personally came up with thousands of suggestions as to what we could do to save money. Everyone took it on. And we reduced costs in the company dramatically. It was just amazing, the kinds of things that happened—purchasing efficiencies to the tune of half a billion dollars.[52]

Cutting people might be the right thing to do, but don't forget that only knowledgeable people can create the solutions you need to succeed in a crisis. Xerox did have to lay some people off, but far fewer than expected because of their ingenious productivity solutions.

A crisis tempts us to take the focus off customers and employees and onto the finances. Getting buried in budgets and balance sheets can lead to mindless cutting rather than focusing on value. For example, one large home-center retailer cut costs by firing most of their experienced full-time staff and replacing them with part-timers. This looked good temporarily on the cash-flow statement, but drastically hurt both employees and customers. Customers had long depended on staff consultants, many of whom were formerly carpenters, plumbers, and electricians. Losing those people meant losing customers as well. By cutting in the wrong places, the big retailer badly undermined itself.[53]

Focusing on customers. By contrast, companies that succeed in unpredictable times focus totally on value. They don't just cut fat; they simplify and reduce complexities that customers don't value or even understand. Typically, a breakthrough company has

> A crisis tempts us to take the focus off customers and employees and onto the finances.

a robust, deliberate campaign of customer retention.[54] They do this by focusing narrowly on the job real customers want them to do.

"We're already doing that job," you say.

Think again. A Bain survey of senior executives in 362 companies found the following:

- Ninety-six percent said their company was customer-focused.

- Eighty percent believed their company delivered a "superior customer experience."

- Eight percent of their customers agreed.[55]

Now, that's a big gap.

You're thinking, "But our customer-satisfaction numbers are good. Our customers are satisfied!"

But you should be asking yourself, "Are they loyal?"

There's a difference between customer satisfaction and customer loyalty. Merely satisfied customers find no reason to complain. Loyal customers, on the other hand, are emotionally connected to you. They represent the biggest share of your business because they repurchase. They would miss you if you were gone.

In a crisis, many companies work hard at cutting costs out of their systems and processes, but it doesn't necessarily follow that customers will find those cuts helpful. As Rosabeth Moss Kanter points out, "Simplification is not the norm, and that's a problem." In a crisis, you need to pack light, and deciding what you pack and what you leave out of the pack should depend on customer value. "We have been paying a price for too much complexity, creating—or allowing—so much variety that it is hard to sort through it, and adding so many loops to the chain that no one feels personal responsibility for the whole system or even comprehends it fully."[56] How often have you been paralyzed by the choices of toothpaste, for example. Tartar control? Whitening? Disease prevention? What if I want a product that will do all of those jobs for me?

> There's a difference between customer satisfaction and customer loyalty.

In most cases, simplification reduces uncertainty. You can get more predictable results if you focus on simple, high-value offerings for the customer. For example, Unilever cut customer confusion by reducing its number of soaps, deodorants, and other products from 1,600 to 200.[57] Similarly, since children (and their parents) hate getting shots, Sanofi-Pasteur has developed a five-in-one vaccine so toddlers can be immunized with one shot instead of several.[58] And knowing that most of their customers hate their complicated monthly cable TV bills, several American television networks have teamed up to offer the hulu.com service—simple, available anytime, and free.

Too many old measures of success live past their usefulness, such as having more products or more stores or more distribution channels than the competition. "The answer is less. Do less than your competitors to beat them. Instead of one-upping, try one-downing. Instead of outdoing, try underdoing."[59] In other words, do more of what customers really care about and less of what they don't.

The principle here is to focus on the job customers really want you to do for them—and that doesn't necessarily mean more of what you've done before. Polaroid went bankrupt in 2001 pushing onto the market dozens of new versions of their instant-film cameras, while Canon and

> Do less than your competitors to beat them.... In other words, do more of what customers really care about and less of what they don't.

other companies prospered by moving into digital photography. Polaroid misinterpreted the job to be done: customers want instant pictures, all right, but not if it means buying expensive and unnecessary film. Canon thrived by doing less—getting out of the analog photography market altogether—and more of what their customers really wanted.

When you're "in the mountains," do more of what is really important and less of what isn't. And what's really important? The answer is simple: Do more of what customers really value. Answer the question, "What job do they really want us to do for them?" Strip out activities that don't contribute to the answer. Companies that are succeeding jettison anything that distracts from retaining customers.

> Even in tough times (perhaps especially in tough times), people want to contribute, they want to help, they want to make a difference.

Focusing on employees. Of course, companies that put the emphasis on the customer enjoy higher levels of customer loyalty. Intriguingly, they also enjoy higher levels of employee loyalty. When times are bad, employees will stay with you, but this doesn't mean they want to. The research shows that when companies "align the customer experience with the employee experience, they create employees who are passionate about what the company stands for. Passion and engagement go hand in hand."[60]

Our research at FranklinCovey shows that people on average are less motivated by money than by the feeling that their contribution is valued.[61] Knowledge workers—the new majority—want meaningful work. Even in tough times (perhaps especially in tough times), people want to contribute, they want to help, they want to make a difference. Perhaps this is why Anne Mulcahy was able to save far more money by asking Xerox people to help her with their ideas than she would have by laying them off.

The leader's task in a crisis is to create a "contribution-focused" workplace. Tell prospective new hires, "Don't ask me for a job—bring me a solution." When staff cuts threaten, be up-front with people: "We're going to be underwater soon unless we can help more customers in ways they will pay for. What big customer problem are we the answer to? What can we contribute?"

A construction company faced with big layoffs went to the workers and said, "Here's the situation. New construction has dried up. We have no cash flow. But we value everyone here and we want to keep you on. What can we do together?"

Hundreds of ideas later, the company was busy again doing green remodeling of existing structures. They were installing low-maintenance plumbing, healthier coats of paint, energy-conserving devices, cold-cathode lighting that draws little electricity and rarely needs replacement, and solar-power panels. The green "do-over" business surged and the company thrived.

How many times have we heard leaders say that people are the organization's most valuable asset? (Of course, on the financial statements, people are a cost, not an asset.) But in a crisis, your people really are your most valuable asset. Unleashing them to help you meet the crisis is only smart business. And when you ask them, "What do you have to give?" most will respond with value. In the end, this is why people stay.

Pushing the "Reset" Button: Aligning the Organization to Customer Value

The steeper the climb, the lighter the pack needs to be. Doing more with less does not mean saying yes to more things. It means saying no to more things and yes to only the most important things.

> Even top performers suffer when their focus is divided.

As we've seen, in a crisis, it's essential to focus the organization more on customer value—the job the customer wants done. Once you have narrowed down the job to be done, your task is to realign the organization to provide that value.

Unfortunately, many companies simply cut people and resources without rethinking the job to be done. According to Watson-Wyatt research, a weak economy "forces companies to do more with less. Supervisors and managers often turn to their top performers, pressuring them to carry more of the productivity burden. The additional stress can cause burnout, disillusionment, and disengagement."

Besides the stress of more work, even top performers suffer when their focus is divided. Research shows that high-engagement employees rate "unclear job definition" as their top stressor.[62] Faced with several jobs to do, they can't excel at any of them and soon "crash and burn." In this respect, people are like airplanes. Airplane crashes are rarely the product of one catastrophic failure. Usually what happens is several smaller things go wrong all at once. The pilot's attention is forced in too many directions and disaster follows.[63]

Finding clarity in the chaos becomes more important than ever. We see organizations with fewer people, fewer resources, more confusion, and more noise—people are simply expected to do as much or more with far fewer resources.

Now you're probably thinking, "It's unavoidable. If we're going to keep the doors open, we're all going to have to suck it up and do more work."

Maybe. But you should also be thinking, "How can we realign ourselves to do the work that really matters?"

What happens when your computer gets overloaded?

It slows down. Everything takes longer. It starts giving you error messages. Soon it freezes. And then it crashes.

When your good people are overloaded, you need to do the same thing you would do with a crashing computer: clean out the clutter and reboot.

> How can we realign ourselves to do the work that really matters?

In turning around Xerox, Anne Mulcahy did not hesitate to "push the reset button." She quickly realigned the organization to true customer priorities.

> Fifty to sixty percent of our people are actually in customer-facing jobs—a lot higher than it used to be. For example, we have focused executive programs where all of our executives "own" customers whom they are responsible for when it comes to communicating, solving problems, getting resources…. Customers always have access to our people and answers to their questions.[64]

Instead of having to do two or three jobs at once, Xerox managers redefined themselves into one job: "owning the customer." If your good people are under high stress and risking burnout, isn't it time to rethink the work and strip down to what is truly essential? Doesn't that make sense?

Apparently not to many organizations. Half of American workers are now putting in more than 50 hours a week. One fourth work all year without a vacation. "The dirty little secret of American productivity: It's the highest in the world only because we put in more hours than anyone else."[65] Not because we are smart and focused on key priorities.

> No one can afford to carry responsibilities that are not core to the team's purpose.

On the mountain, "packing light" means dropping things that are not absolutely essential to the climb. In the organization, a smart focus on key priorities has to come down to the level of each team and individual worker. No one can afford to carry responsibilities that are not core to the team's purpose. This means there must be absolute alignment across the organization as to what is core and what isn't.

Anne Mulcahy reflects: "When people ask me how this company made so much progress so quickly, I think they want to hear that there was something particularly brilliant about the strategy or the planning. The reality is: it was the alignment of the people around a common set of goals."[66]

So is everyone on the team "packing light" and headed for the summit? Probably not. One of the new realities we live with is that knowledge workers make their own decisions about how to spend their time. Unlike the industrial workers of the past, knowledge workers to a great extent decide for themselves what to work on from moment to moment.

Now is the time to reset your culture from "slow and heavy" to "lean and mean." FranklinCovey research shows there's plenty of room for a reset:

- Only 9 percent of workers feel a very high level of commitment to organizational goals.

- Only 22 percent agree that there is a clear line of sight between their own work and the organization's top priorities.

- They spend 23 percent of their time on "urgent but irrelevant activities."

- They spend 17 percent of their time on "counter-productive activities."[67]

A crisis is an opportunity to push the reset button and start doing more of those things that really matter. Listen once more to Erik Weihenmayer, the champion mountain climber, who knows something about adversity:

> It's a great time to examine your priorities and ask yourself what life you really want to create. It's time to make those hard choices, to scale down your distractions, to take a hard look at your losses and see if there's a nugget that can propel you forward and make a change in your life that you've wanted to do anyway and been too scared or too slow to do it.[68]

The following "More With Less" planning tool might help.

"More With Less" Plan

This planning tool will help you pinpoint the actions you need to take now to increase the productivity of your team.

Build Customer Loyalty

Answer these questions to pinpoint how you can provide more customer value:

> Who are your team's most important customers (internal and/or external)?

> What are these customers' most important goals?

> What specific jobs are your customers hiring your team to do?

Align the Organization to Customer Value

Now that you've clarified the job your customers want you to do for them, answer these questions to align yourself to accomplish that job:

> What should we start doing in order to help our customers achieve their most important goals?

> What should we stop doing because it's not relevant to our customers' most important goals?

Achieve More With Less

Given your answers to the preceding questions, fill out this commitment to achieve more with less:

We serve [key customers]

by [doing this job]

to help them achieve [their most important goals].

To achieve more for our customers, we will spend less time and resources on [systems, processes, or tasks that do not add value to the customer]

and we will tightly focus our remaining time and resources on [systems, processes, and tasks that add value to the customer].

Teach to Learn

The best way to learn is to teach. It's a commonplace that the teacher learns far more than the student. If you really want to internalize the insights you've learned in this chapter, in the next day or so, find someone—a co-worker, a friend, a family member—and teach him or her those insights. Ask the provocative questions here or come up with your own.

- In uncertain times, everyone is challenged to do more with less. But what does "more with less" really mean? Does it mean trying to do everything you did before, but with fewer people? You say you're doing more with less—but more of what?

- A crisis takes our focus off customers and onto the financials. What are the risks of this shift in focus?

- How is customer loyalty different from customer satisfaction?

- Which customers would miss your organization if it were gone? Why?

- What more could you do for your loyal customers to ensure that "they would miss you if you were gone"?

- What could you stop doing that doesn't contribute to building customer loyalty?

- When layoffs strike, the remaining people usually get assigned additional responsibilities. What are the risks of that?

- What's the difference between "doing more work" and "producing more value"?

- How could you get your team aligned to producing more value instead of just doing more work?

4

Reduce Fear

*Our world is dominated by the extreme,
the unknown, and the very improbable.*
—Nassim Nicholas Taleb

"In the mountains," fear is the great enemy.

Threatened jobs, disintegrating retirement, mortgage problems, high prices, eroding health care—it's all "piling on" people. Economic recession produces a debilitating psychological recession. What *The Economist* calls "an endless series of hobgoblins" takes its toll. Your valued people are not immune to this perfect storm of fear.

Actually, any major change produces fear, such as new strategies, industry fragmentation, or disruptive technologies.

So here are a few provocative questions:

- What does the psychological recession cost you?

- Is your organization fatally distracted by fear? Are people paralyzed by uncertainty?

- Have you figured out how to redirect all this anxiety into productive energy?

What Does the Psychological Recession Cost You?

The costs of fear are heavy. Even in normal times, "distractions consume as much as 28 percent of the average U.S. worker's day…and sap productivity to the tune of $650 billion a year."[69] In these confusing times, people are more mentally sidetracked than ever. When their homes, their families, their jobs, and their health are threatened, it's just plain harder for people to focus.

Of course, if we take the long view, there are no predictable times. Within recent memory, we have seen huge surges in global stock markets and huge collapses. The collapse of the Asian markets, the Dotcom Bubble, the Enron/WorldCom debacle, the September 11 attacks, Middle East wars, near total paralysis of world financial markets—obviously, we do not live in a smooth, predictable world. As Nassim Taleb says, "History does not crawl, it jumps."

But this recognition doesn't help much when you're afraid. And that fear is not irrational when the indicators of uncertainty are high.[70] The resulting psychological recession causes people to disengage mentally from their work at just the time you need their full engagement.

"Fear wears us out, and it undermines our health and well-being. When that happens, we're less able to hope," says Shane Lopez, a researcher into the psychology of hope. "Managing this fear has to happen in a big way at the beginning of a crisis, and then it needs to be mini-managed every day."[71]

Is Your Organization Fatally Distracted by Fear? Are People Paralyzed by Uncertainty?

So how do you manage fear?

Olivier Blanchard, chief economist of the International Monetary Fund, advises leaders to give absolutely clear direction. "First and foremost, reduce uncertainty…. Above all, adopt clear policies and act decisively."[72]

With a clear, unmistakable mission, people can transform anxiety into action and productivity.

When an airliner en route from New York City to Charlotte, North Carolina, U.S.A., made a crash landing in the freezing Hudson River on a January afternoon, there was none of the shrieking panic among passengers that you might see in the movies. People all over the world were fascinated by the iconic photo of 155 people standing calmly on the wings of the sinking airplane waiting to be rescued.

> With a clear, unmistakable mission, people can transform anxiety into action and productivity.

But experts were not surprised. In plane crashes, as in any major disaster, people tend to respond quietly. When the plane crashed, "people were calm—the pervading sound was not screaming, but silence, which is very typical," according to Amanda Ripley, a researcher on how people deal with crisis.

"You don't hear the mayhem and hysteria that we would expect," says Ripley. "That doesn't mean people aren't frightened. It means…they are waiting for direction."

The pilot's plainspoken directions to the passengers were exactly what the situation required. He told them the problem straight out and instructed them how to deal with it.

> The thing he did that is particularly important…he warned people. Sometimes you get pilots or crew who don't want to tell the passengers what's going on because they don't want them to freak out. But any warning, even as short as that, can really put you in the right mind frame. We know people are so obedient in disasters, so it's really helpful to get that kind of command.[73]

Even if they're not sure what to do, leaders can defuse a lot of fear just by communicating clearly about the situation. In crisis time, "communication carries more significance and requires greater transparency."[74] And yet only 13 percent of leaders have talked to their people about the turbulent times we live in. Nearly half of respondents say that their "leaders have taken no actions to respond to the economic anxiety in the workplace."[75]

What do you say to lower anxiety levels?

Be transparent and simply tell the story. Don't assume everybody already knows how the turbulence is affecting the organization. All they hear is news about downturns and layoffs, so they need to hear exactly how the firm is doing—

> Leaders can defuse a lot of fear just by communicating clearly about the situation.

and they need to hear it often. Tell the story about where you are, what the numbers are, and what the impact will be. Be clear about reality and don't fall into the trap of sounding more optimistic than you should.

Talk about what's next. If you have a strategy, lay it out in clear terms. (If you don't, say so and ask for help.) Describe what has to happen and what everyone's role must be. Give people the chance to share their feelings, concerns and, most of all, their ideas.[76]

In his analysis of leadership in uncertain times, Ram Charan relates this story. Like most other companies, chemical giant E. I. DuPont de Nemours suffered in the downturn of 2008–2009. Focused on reducing fear, DuPont calmed nerves among their tens of thousands of employees by communicating reality and a clear strategic direction. The firm's finance leaders explained in plain terms how the crisis was affecting DuPont and advised employees on how to safeguard their $18 billion in retirement funds.

Within 10 days, every single DuPont employee had met face to face with a manager to hear the firm's strategy and the employee's role in carrying it out. Employees were asked for their three top ideas to preserve cash. Not long afterwards, the firm surveyed employees to find out if they had understood the message: Were they scared, or were they energized and ready to confront the crisis?[77]

Historically, DuPont has a remarkable focus for such a large organization: a typical DuPont employee is 50 percent more likely than the average American worker to know the organization's direction and priorities.[78]

Clarity reduces fear, even if what is made clear isn't very positive. A first guideline for leaders is to talk straight and listen with empathy to the concerns of the team. In a time of massive collective fear, INSEAD Professor Quy Huy advises leaders "to instill collective calm conducive to creative reflection and thoughtful action, as opposed to collective panic…. It is precisely in these emotionally volatile and challenging times that leaders show their mettle, or their lack of it." [79]

Have You Figured Out How to Redirect All This Anxiety Into Productive Energy?

Clear direction can go a long way toward reducing fear. But the roots of fear still remain. Like a weedy vine, fear comes up from under the surface and saps emotional energy that could be used productively. It's not enough to ignore it or tell ourselves to snap out of it. An effective leader uproots it.

To do that, you have to recognize that fear is an emotional response. As a leader, you're now in the business of managing other people's emotions. And that's tough, because "managers are taught to manage action, not emotions behind actions."[80]

You successfully uproot debilitating fear by changing the paradigms that produce fear. You don't do it by exhorting people to get over it or to walk straight into the storm. It will crush them—privately, silently perhaps, but inevitably. If you really want to help people, you don't work on their behavior, you work on their paradigms.

The Root of Fear

The paradigm at the root of the psychological recession is the widespread belief that people have no control over what happens to them. The forces of change are so crushing that people simply wilt. What Martin Seligman calls "learned helplessness" is a psychological condition in which people act helpless, even when they have the power to change the unpleasant or even harmful circumstance.[81]

What's the consequence? A feeling of futility causes people to disengage from their work. They see themselves as victims of the economy, of the company, of their co-workers, of an unfair boss, or of the "system." Judith Bardwick describes it this way:

> A psychological recession is an emotional state in which people feel extremely vulnerable to economic hardship, leading to a dour view of the present and an even bleaker view of the future, which often is not based on current reality. This gloomy mindset reinforces people's perception of the world as a risky place in which they have little or no control. Anxiety, depression, and a sense of being powerless are a poisonous mix.[82]

Your task as a leader is to help people uproot this mindset, and the only way to do that is to replace it with another mindset. Martin Seligman says, "Habits of thinking need not be forever...individuals can choose the way they think."

> "Learned helplessness" is a psychological condition in which people act helpless, even when they have the power to change.

Work within your Circle of Influence, not your Circle of Concern. Everybody has worries ranging all over the place—job, family, the national debt, the possibility of a comet hitting the earth. We call this range of worries the "Circle of Concern." Typically, we separate immediate concerns from remote concerns. But in a frighteningly unpredictable world, remote concerns become immediate. We see institutions we counted on coming down around us. We feel caught up in a global economic tailspin.

If our mindset is to focus all our energies on the Circle of Concern, we become passive, reactive, unable to respond except as victims. But there are some things over which we have no real control and others that we can do something about. We could identify those concerns in the latter group by circumscribing them within a smaller Circle of Influence.[83]

So the trick is to shift your mindset from the Circle of Concern to the Circle of Influence. By doing so, you become proactive—taking charge of your own future, exercising your own resourcefulness and initiative. Within the Circle of Influence are those measures you can take to tame unpredictability. By focusing your time and energy on the Circle of Influence, your power to control your future increases.

Consider the success of Amazon.com founder Jeff Bezos. When he started the company in his garage in 1994, he believed that controlled growth was better than the wild ride other companies were taking during the Dotcom Boom. He was completely transparent about what he could control and what he couldn't. He knew that his company would not be profitable for a long time, and made that clear to his shareholders. (His vision for his business—at first it was just an online bookstore—required heavy capitalization and borrowing.)

What Bezos wanted to do was to construct in a carefully controlled way the biggest retailer on the planet. That's why he called it "Amazon," after the biggest river on the planet, which nevertheless starts as a tiny rivulet in the Andes Mountains. That little stream of books from a warehouse in Seattle has become a mighty flood of products of every kind, but Bezos had to channel it vigilantly to make it so.

Bezos worked carefully within his Circle of Influence. He watched meticulously over those aspects of the business that really mattered to customers, paying no attention to the encircling chaos of the Internet "gold rush." Surrounded by dotcom disasters, poorly capitalized and conceptualized businesses that spiraled out of control by the thousands, he stayed inside that circle. In a notoriously out-of-control industry where others were making vast fortunes and then losing them overnight, he still stayed inside that circle. As he grew, he honed the minutiae of his delivery process with great care to make it fast, faultless, inexpensive, and "seamless"—his favorite word. The mantra: "Make it easy and make it cheap" until it's as simple as "one click."

> Anytime we think the problem is "out there," that thought is the problem.

The company finally turned a profit in 2001. Eight years later, Bezos vaulted his greatest hurdle in the midst of the severest recession in decades: Amazon became debt-free.

By concentrating on your Circle of Influence, you automatically buck the unpredictability factor. You focus on what is predictable. Anytime we think the problem is "out there," that very thought is the problem. We empower what's out there to control us. The paradigm is "outside in"—what's out there has to change before we can change.

But the proactive approach is to change from the inside out: we can be more resourceful, we can be more diligent, we can be more creative, we can be more cooperative.[84]

What's "out there" cannot by its very nature be controlled. You can control only what's in you, as the story of Amazon.com strikingly demonstrates.

And most certainly, you cannot control other people.

This is one of the most serious mistakes leaders can make, and is another primary source of fear in the workplace.

Adopt a "Knowledge Age" Paradigm of Leadership. Many leaders still hold an "Industrial Age" paradigm of leadership. To the Industrial Age leader, people are like machines to be efficiently controlled. Supervisors stand over them to ensure closer and closer compliance with orders from the top down. It's a work environment where the consequences of stepping out of line are fearful.

Why does this kind of environment generate fear in people? What kinds of fears? Fear of loss, primarily—loss of job, personal dignity, security, status, or self-esteem. Perhaps even more deeply, they fear the meaninglessness that comes from being treated as a mindless cog in a machine rather than as a creative, thinking, purposeful human being.

In a sense, the Industrial Age was about getting predictable results—the same car, tool, teacup, or toaster—every time. The irony? In the quest to banish unpredictability, leaders ended up driving out what is most essential in unpredictable times: the ability to adapt. The rigid control mindset of the Industrial Age led to the death of the initiative and resourcefulness an organization needs to survive in a world dominated by the extreme, the unknown, and the very improbable. And we have seen the consequences, as Industrial Age company after company slides into history.

A far more effective paradigm is "Knowledge Age" leadership. In the Knowledge Age, people are valued for their unique contribution—their ability to learn, to adapt, to innovate, to capture opportunities entrepreneurially. They are no longer just machines to be switched on and off and discarded on schedule. To lead in the Knowledge Age, you need a paradigm of releasing, unleashing, valuing the different (even disruptive) viewpoint. You motivate people with zeal for the mission.

> In the quest to banish unpredictability, leaders ended up driving out what is most essential in unpredictable times: the ability to adapt

When Hurricane Katrina hit the state of Mississippi in the U.S.A., it nearly destroyed much of its electrical power grid. The storm ripped up power lines in most of the southern half of the state. Nearly 200,000 people were without electricity. The headquarters of Mississippi Power was in ruins and its disaster response center flooded. The most optimistic estimate for restoring power was one month.

The day before the crisis, Melvin Wilson was a marketing manager for Mississippi Power. The next day, he was in charge of "storm logistics," responsible for the 11,000-person crew whose job was to clean up and restore electricity to thousands of homes and businesses. Four-fifths of the crew didn't even work for Mississippi Power—they were brought in from other regions of the country to help with the emergency. According to *USA Today*:

> Wilson needed nurses, beds, meals, tetanus shots, laundry service, showers, toilets, and much more— and he needed them now. And he needed double the quantities called for in the company's "worst-case scenario." And he needed them in places that had no electricity, no plumbing, no phones, few road signs, and sporadic looting. The fact that Wilson didn't have a working phone was his tough luck; if he failed, men would go hungry, hospitals would stay dark, and the suffering of his community would endure. "My day job did not prepare me for this," says Wilson, his voice choked with emotion, recalling the burden of having 11,000 mouths to feed.

Wilson and his team did the job, and they did it in less than half the projected time. Twelve days after the storm, power was restored across the state of Mississippi.

How did they do it?

Well, they couldn't have done it a few years before. Emergency response used to be handled from the top down, with orders flowing from headquarters. Crews in the field waited to be told what to do.

Today everything is different. Line crews make their own decisions, scavenging and purchasing what they need to do the job. One team extracted a generator from an ice-making machine to power up an electrical substation. Faced with price gougers who wanted an exorbitant amount of money to set up showers and beds, the crew built their own shower tents. Unable to buy enough fuel for their repair trucks, crews simply bartered for diesel; they restored electricity to a refinery and a pipeline in exchange for a steady supply of fuel. The mission was to get the power back on—and they exceeded every expectation in achieving that mission.

"Line crews were hanging wire, sticking poles, replacing transformers, and fixing substations at a rate never seen before," said Anthony Topazi, then president of Mississippi Power.

What is even more startling about this level of teamwork is the selflessness involved. Crew members did all these things in full knowledge that their own homes were flooded and their own families in distress.

What had transformed Mississippi Power from a passive, top-down organization that would have been overwhelmed by this crisis, to a proactive, decisive organization that exceeded all expectations in the crisis?

The firm had adopted a mindset of unleashing people instead of reining them in. "Mississippi Power had steeped its culture in…*The 7 Habits of Highly Effective People.*" Principles such as "win–win" and "Be Proactive" worked as a "lubricant to quick action and on-the-spot innovation," according to news reports.[85] Every associate had learned the principles of effectiveness, and company leaders had embraced those principles by freeing people to contribute their best efforts.

Trust is the highest form of human motivation. Mississippi Power trusted people to do what the job required without being told what to do. The company had adopted an entirely new paradigm of leadership.

- They had moved from an Industrial Age paradigm of control to a Knowledge Age paradigm of release.

- They had moved from a paradigm that people are interchangeable and easily replaced, to a paradigm that people have unique talent and ingenuity that the firm had never tapped before.

- They had moved from a focus on methods to a focus on results. Instead of telling people how to do the job, leaders trusted them to think for themselves. No more intimidating supervisors; leaders became resources to the people on the front line whose task was to get the job done.

The key is to replace fear-based management with leadership that unleashes people to make their own contribution, changing the nature of the relationship. The worker becomes his or her own boss, governed by a conscience that contains the commitment to agreed-upon desired results. But it also releases the worker's creative energies toward doing whatever is necessary in harmony with correct principles to achieve those desired results.[86]

> Trust is the highest form of human motivation.

Mississippi Power's response to the crisis of Katrina demonstrates that people are far more motivated by a significant mission than by salary or survival or fear of the boss. The psychologist Abraham Maslow believed that basic survival is first in the hierarchy of human needs, with "self-actualization"—fulfillment of a high purpose—last in the hierarchy.[87] But people will do extraordinary things in the service of an important mission, even when more basic needs are in peril. Conscience drives them; their creative energies surface. People conquer their own fears when the mission matters and they have been entrusted with it.

Mississippi Power President Topazi says, "Before, during, and after the hurricane, our people maintained a sense of direction and focus in spite of personal loss. They demonstrated organizational greatness, follow-through, teamwork, and individual effectiveness—qualities that reflect the basis of Dr. Covey's principles."[88]

Too many organizations suffer with a hangover from the Industrial Age. People are treated as things, as so many interchangeable parts, as simply an unavoidable cost on the balance sheet. Their minds and hearts are not respected as sources of solutions and commitment. They live in fear of losing their future if they don't "toe the line" and do what they're told. The danger: in a crisis, leaders are tempted to lapse even further back into the Industrial Age control paradigm and intensify the atmosphere of fear.

> People conquer their own fears when the mission matters and they have been entrusted with it.

Why should reducing fear be a top priority for you in dealing with the crisis?

Because it's key to getting predictable results in unpredictable times.

If the mission is significant enough, you won't have fearful people working at it. Ironically, the more rigid the controls, the more fear you generate and the less likely you are to achieve your mission. It's almost counterintuitive, but true, that when talented, energetic, ingenious people are unleashed to achieve a high mission, they will find the way to achieve it. You can trust them. You don't need to worry about them.

And that's predictable.

"Reducing Fear" Plan

This planning tool will help you pinpoint the actions you need to take now to reduce fear and increase the engagement of your team. Take time with each question. Pose the questions to your boss, your team, and your peers in the organization.

- What are we focusing on in our Circle of Concern that is outside of our control and wasting our energies?

- What could we focus on in our Circle of Influence that would make the most difference to our future?

- What practices, systems, or processes are left over from the Industrial Age?

- What can we do to replace those practices, systems, and processes to move into the Knowledge Age?

Teach to Learn

The best way to learn is to teach. It's a commonplace that the teacher learns far more than the student. If you really want to internalize the insights you've learned in this chapter, in the next day or so, find someone—a co-worker, a friend, a family member—and teach him or her those insights. Ask the provocative questions here or come up with your own.

- Why do economic troubles cause a "psychological recession"? What do you think that term means?

- What kinds of fears do people suffer from in a turbulent economy?

- What are the costs to people and organizations of a "psychological recession"?

- What can leaders do to help people overcome their fears in turbulent times?

- What is the role of a clear mission and direction in overcoming fear?

- What would you want your leaders to share with you in a crisis?

- What do leaders sometimes do to generate more fear instead of reducing it?

- What are the consequences of exercising too much control over people?

- How would you banish fear on your team?

Conclusion

*It might be unthinkable that we can grasp, from
what seems a very dangerous and unstable world, a
prosperous, stable, and a better future. We can.*
—Joshua Cooper Ramo

A few closing thoughts.

In the Tour de France, the race is won in the mountains.

In the same way, whether in business, education, or government, the successful organization is the one that gets predictably good results in uncertain times.

Consider the case of two camera makers.

Both Polaroid and Canon were giants in consumer photography. And a few years ago, they both hit "the mountains"—the disruptive technology of digital cameras.

In the 1990s, Polaroid looked like a big winner. Their time-honored instant camera was the razor, the film the razor blades. A flood of new models boosted sales—a Barbie camera for girls, a Business Pro camera for the office, and the I-Zone for teens, among others. The old business model of virtually giving away inexpensive cameras to make big profits on expensive film never looked better.

By 2001, Polaroid was bankrupt. Share price had fallen nearly 100 percent, from $60 in 1997 to 28 cents. All remaining assets were sold off.[89]

By contrast, Canon moved systematically into digital photography in the late 1990s and thrived. In 2001, Canon issued its first mass-market digital cameras—inexpensive, reliable, and independent of the film business. The cameras were a hit. Share values rose predictably, as Canon shares had pretty much always done since the day Goro Yoshida sold his first "Kwannon" camera in Japan in 1933.

In the midst of the 2008–09 recession, a Canon share was worth twice what it was in 1997 at the height of the technology boom. Even while suffering a drastic slowdown in sales, Canon's profit margins far exceeded those of its competitors. Year after year, it is voted "the most trusted brand" in cameras across Eurasia and the United States.[90]

Why does one team collapse "in the mountains" and another chug predictably forward to win?

The principles of success in the mountains are time-tested and never really change:

- Execute priorities with excellence.
- Move with the speed of trust.
- Achieve more with less.
- Reduce fear.

Teams who don't live by these principles inevitably fall out of the race when the terrain gets tough. They lose sight of their strategic priorities. They lose the momentum that comes from having trusted teammates, systems, and processes. They lose focus on the job to be done. And finally, they lose confidence in themselves.

Polaroid charged into the mountains at full speed. At first, they were actually ahead of others in developing digital photography, but the lack of internal clarity about the company's business model led to fatal delays in execution. Digital development slowed and was starved of investment. In the confusion about priorities, Polaroid lost sight of what customers really wanted. The old business model based on sales of film made the customer's life more costly and complicated. Once digital cameras eliminated the need for film, consumers dropped Polaroid almost overnight.

To make things worse, Polaroid's top management lost the trust of employees by taking substantial bonuses while the workforce was being cut in half.[91] The final blow was the collapse of technology stocks in 2000. As fear spread through the markets in the wake of the bust, Polaroid simply crumpled.

Canon entered the same mountains—the disruptive shift to digital technology—at the same time. But their story was very different. They looked not only at what customers were trying to do, but also at the experience they were having. Realizing that the digital platform was far simpler for the customer, Canon dedicated a division to building the digital-camera business model, with full, shared understanding of the strategy. Eventually, as many anticipated, the division became the business.[92]

Internally, Canon builds trust with its *sanbun-setsu* (three-portion) system of sharing profits first with employees, then with investors and management. The company also bolsters employee loyalty with its three time-honored management "pillars": "Competency-Based Promotion, Top Priority to Health, and Family Comes First."[93] Because of its track record of predictable excellent results regardless of the economic environment, Canon remains a top choice in the capital markets. Customers, employees, and investors look to the future with confidence.

So, what about your team? Are you more like Polaroid or Canon? Are you poised to get predictable results—no matter how unpredictable the times?

Ask yourself the following thought questions about the team or work group you belong to. Put a check mark in the box that applies.

	Yes	No
Does every team member know exactly what the team goals are?		
Does every team member know what his/her role is in achieving those goals?		
Does every team member know the score? In other words, does everybody know what the measures of success are and where the team is in relation to those measures?		
Do team members meet regularly and frequently (at least weekly) to account to each other for progress on team goals?		
Are you actively "moving the middle"—helping everyone move toward the performance levels of your best performers?		
Is repeat business a high percentage of your revenues?		
Do you have a low employee-turnover rate for your industry?		
Are you confident you're doing the job your customers really want you to do for them?		
Do your customers have a simple, streamlined experience with you?		
Are team members so energized by the mission that they are undeterred by fear and anxiety?		
Total Yes/No		
TOTAL SCORE = # of yeses		

SCORE	
9–10	You're well positioned to get predictable results, regardless of the times.
7–8	You're going to get uneven results in tough times.
5–6	Your team will have a bumpy ride through turbulent times.
3–4	Your survival is seriously in doubt.
0–2	Remember to turn off the lights and close the door on your way out.

In all candor, if you answered no to any of the questions above, you risk serious trouble "in the mountains." You'll be outrun by those who execute with excellence, who are highly trusted, who do more of what the customer really needs done, and who engage employees in a meaningful purpose they can believe in.

The times are, by their nature, unpredictable. You can't begin to compute all the uncertainties of the future into a set of certainties. But there are certain principles you can rely on even in volatile times:

- You can pack only a few things in the mountains—so they'd better be important things.

- You'll be trusted only as far as you are worthy of trust.

- If customers really must have what you sell, they'll find a way to pay for it.

- The only thing stronger than fear is purpose—so make your purpose strong.

Those principles will never let you down.

Notes

1. We are aware of the doping scandals surrounding the Tour de France and other events like the Olympics. We certainly do not approve of cheating in any form, including doping. Of course, we do not know all the facts. Still, we find the example of expert cycling teams "in the mountains" helpful in understanding success under extreme and unpredictable conditions.

2. "Succeeding in the New Economic Environment," *Report of the IBM Institute for Business Value*, Mar. 2009, p. 12.

3. IBM Institute Report, p. 4.

4. "Riding in Fast Company: Lance Armstrong and Team USPS," *Fast Company*, Feb. 8, 2008.

5. "CEO Challenge 2008: Top 10 Challenges," *Report of the Conference Board*, Nov. 2008, p. 5.

6. *FranklinCovey xQ Database Averages*, Dec. 31, 2008; "The Execution Quotient," FranklinCovey white paper, Mar. 3, 2004. FranklinCovey's xQ Survey has helped 150,000 people in thousands of organizations pinpoint ways to improve their execution discipline.

7. Erika Herb, et al., "Teamwork at the Top," *McKinsey Quarterly*, Aug. 2002.

8. IBM Institute Report, p. 12.

9. Robert S. Kaplan and David P. Norton, "Strategy Execution Needs a System," *HarvardBusiness.org Voices*, Apr. 20, 2009.

10. "The Crash of Eastern Airlines 401," http://eastern401.googlepages.com/home.

11. Orit Gadiesh and Hugh MacArthur, *Lessons from Private Equity Any Company Can Use.* Harvard Business Press, 2008, p. 16.

12. John W. Miller, "Maersk: Container Ship Cuts Costs to Stay Afloat," *The Wall Street Journal*, Apr. 8, 2009.

13. A. P. Moller-Maersk A/S, Annual Report 2008.

14. *FranklinCovey xQ Database Averages.*

15. "Maersk Container Industry Case Study," FranklinCovey Center for Advanced Research, http://franklincoveyresearch.org/documents/textsearch?criteria=maersk.

16. Nassim Nicholas Taleb, *The Black Swan: The Impact of the Highly Improbable,* New York: Random House, 2007, p. 204.

17. Gadiesh and MacArthur, p. 19.

18. *Everest: Taking the Team to the Summit,* FranklinCovey InSights video.

19. Gadiesh and MacArthur, p. 24.

20. Brion O'Connor, "American Flyers," *ESPN,* http://sports.espn.go.com/espnmag/story?section=magazine&id=3742027.

21. "Driving Business Results Through Continuous Engagement," *2008/2009 WorkUSA Survey Report*, Watson Wyatt Worldwide, 2009, p. 1.

22. "The Economic Impact of the Achievement Gap in America's Schools: Summary of Findings," *McKinsey Quarterly*, April 2009.

23. Thomas Friedman, "Swimming Without a Suit," *The New York Times*, Apr. 21, 2009.

24. Bill Amelio, "Navigating the Downturn," *INSEAD Knowledge*, April 2009.

25. David L. Cooperrider and Diana Whitney, *Appreciative Inquiry: A Positive Revolution in Change*, Berrett-Koehler, 2005.

26. Stephen R. Covey, "8th Habit Leadership: Unleashing Potential," *Chief Learning Officer* Oct. 2005.

27. Gautam Naik, "Hospital Races to Learn Lessons of Ferrari Pit Stop," *The Wall Street Journal*, Nov. 14, 2006.

28. *Speed Up Your Team: Continuously Improving Team Processes*, FranklinCovey InSights video.

29. "Trust in Governments, Corporations, and Global Institutions Continues to Decline," Global Survey of the World Economic Forum, Dec. 15, 2005. Conference Board Report, p. 5.

30. Stephen M. R. Covey, *The Speed of Trust: The One Thing That Changes Everything*, Free Press, 2006, pp. 17, 19.

31. IBM Institute Report, p. 3.

32. "Michael Schumacher—The Best Driver in the Car Racing Sport, a Legend in His Own Lifetime," *German Culture Magazine*, http://www.germanculture.com.ua/library/weekly/michael-schumacher.htm.

33. David Tremayne, "Flawed Genius Schumacher Calls Time on Brilliant Career," *The Independent*, Sep. 11, 2006.

34. Stephen M. R. Covey, "Daring to Trust Again," interview by Newton Holt, *Associations Now*, Jul. 2007.

35. Terry Macalister, "Full of Beans: Howard Schultz, Chairman of Starbucks," *The Guardian*, Oct. 16, 2004.

36. Stephen M. R. Covey, "Daring."

37. Stephen M. R. Covey, "Daring."

38. Betsy Morris, "The Accidental CEO," *Fortune*, Jun. 9, 2003, p. 45.

39. "2008 Chief Executive of the Year," ChiefExecutive.net. http://www.chiefexecutive.net/ME2/dirmod.asp?sid=&nm =&type=Publishing&mod=Publications%3A%3AArticle& mid=8F3A7027421841978F18BE895F87F791&tier=4&id= 01425EF8AE72494B9D15BDDCEC6C5733.

40. Don Tennant, "Anne Mulcahy on Getting the Color Back into Xerox," *CIO*, Jun. 17, 2008.

41. Stephen M. R. Covey, "The Speed of Trust Tour," speech delivered in San Francisco at the Sir Francis Drake Hotel, April 30, 2009.

42. "Wall Street's Latest Crisis of Leadership," *BusinessWeek*, Oct. 3, 2008.

43. "Alpharetta-based Integrity Bank Fails," *The Atlanta Journal-Constitution*, Aug. 29, 2008.

44. Quy Huy, "Leadership in Crisis," *INSEAD Knowledge*, http://knowledge.insead.edu/LeadershipinCrisis081216. cfm?vid=156.

45. Patricia Aburdene, *Megatrends 2010: The Rise of Conscious Capitalism*, Hampton Roads, 2007, p. 27.

46. Rosabeth Moss Kanter, "The Value of Role Models in the Downturn," *HarvardBusiness.org Voices*, Mar. 2, 2009.

47. FranklinCovey-HarrisInteractive "Trust Quotient" Survey Results of 12,000 American Workers, available from FranklinCovey.

48. Erik Weihenmayer, "Touch the Top," podcast April 13, 2009. http://www.touchthetop.com/press/press.htm#04- 13-09-2.

49. Anne M. Mulcahy, "From the Podium," MIT Leadership Center, http://sloanleadership.mit.edu/r-mulcahy.php.

50. "Crisis Helped to Reshape Xerox in Positive Ways," *Knowledge@Wharton*, Nov. 16, 2005.

51. Gianna Englert, "Anne Mulcahy," http://www. capitalistchicks.com/?q=node/237. Accessed Apr 29, 2009.

52. "Crisis," *Knowledge@Wharton*.

53. Rita McGrath, "A Better Way to Cut Costs," *Harvard-Business.org Voices*, Mar. 9, 2009.

54. IBM Institute Report, pp. 6–7.

55. James Allen, Frederick Reichheld, and Barney Hamilton, "The Three 'Ds' of Customer Experience," *Harvard Management Update*, Nov. 7, 2005.

56. Rosabeth Moss Kanter, "Simplicity: The Next Big Thing," *HarvardBusiness.org Voices*, Feb. 12, 2009.

57. C. Crum, et al., *Demand Management Best Practices*, J. Ross Publishing, 2003.

58. "Top 10 Medical Breakthroughs of 2008," *Time Magazine*, http://www.time.com/time/specials/2008/top10/article/0,30583,1855948_1863993_1864002,00.html.

59. Pete Cashmore, "Recession Is the Mother of Tech Invention," *Mashable: The Social Media Guide*. http://mashable.com/2008/10/12/recession-is-the-mother-of-tech-invention. Accessed April 20, 2009.

60. Watson Wyatt Worldwide Report, p. 19.

61. *FranklinCovey xQ Database Averages.*

62. Watson Wyatt Worldwide Report, p. 23.

63. Malcolm Gladwell, *Outliers: The Story of Success*, Little, Brown, 2008, p.183

64. "Crisis," *Knowledge@Wharton*.

65. Chuck Salter, "Solving the Real Productivity Crisis," *Fast Company*, Dec. 19, 2007.

66. "From the Podium," MIT Center.

67. "The Execution Quotient: The Measure of What Matters. A FranklinCovey White Paper." FranklinCovey Center for Advanced Research.

68. Weihenmayer, "Touch the Top."

69. Maggie Jackson, "May We Have Your Attention, Please?" *BusinessWeek*, Jun. 12, 2008.

70. Olivier Blanchard, "Nearly Nothing to Fear but Fear Itself," *The Economist*, Jan. 29, 2009.

71. Jennifer Robison, "What if the Recession Endures?" *Gallup Management Journal*, April 2, 2009.

72. Olivier Blanchard, *The Economist*.

73. Gary Hershorn, "Survival Lessons from a Sinking Plane," Reuters News Service, Jan. 16, 2009.

74. Robison, *Gallup Management Journal*.

75. "Economic Anxiety Poll Results," *Elliott Masie's Learning Trends*, Oct. 1, 2008.

76. John Baldoni, "How to Talk to Your Employees About the Recession," *HarvardBusiness.org Voices*, Apr. 29, 2009.

77. Ram Charan, *Leadership in the Era of Economic Uncertainty,* McGraw-Hill, 2008.

78. *FranklinCovey xQ Database Averages.*

79. Quy Huy, "Leadership in Crisis," *INSEAD Knowledge Base.*

80. James McIntosh, "Nonsense at Work," *Fast Company,* Feb. 16, 2009.

81. Martin Seligman, *Helplessness: On Depression, Development, and Death,* San Francisco: W. H. Freeman, 1975.

82. Abstract of Judith M. Bardwick, *One Foot Out the Door,* AMACOM, 2007.

83. Stephen R. Covey, *The 7 Habits of Highly Effective People,* Simon & Schuster, 1989, p. 82.

84. Covey, *7 Habits*, p. 88

85. Dennis Cauchon, "The Little Company That Could," *USA Today*, Oct. 9, 2005.

86. Covey, *7 Habits*, p. 178.

87. Abraham H. Maslow, "A Theory of Human Motivation," *Psychological Review*, v. 50, pp. 370–396.

88. "FranklinCovey Presents Leadership Greatness Award to Mississippi Power," *SouthernCompany Media Room*, http://southerncompany.mediaroom.com/index.php?s=43&item=173. Accessed April 30, 2009.

89. S. M. Chung, "Polaroid Goes Bankrupt, Plans to Sell Existing Assets," *The Tech Online Edition*, Oct. 23, 2001.

90. "Canon Most Trusted Brand," *ePhotozine,* Mar. 6, 2009; "Canon USA Honored with #1 Ranking in Brandweek's Customer Loyalty Survey," *Business Wire*, Jun. 13, 2006 and Feb. 26, 2009.

91. Michael K. Ozanian, "Out of Focus," *Forbes*, Jan. 22, 2001.

92. Graham Hill, "Harness Your Best Customers to Drive Successful Innovation," mycustomer.com. Accessed May 11, 2009.

93. "Canon Camera Story," http://www.canon.com/camera-museum/history/canon_story/1937_1945/1937_1945.html. Accessed May 28, 2009.

Index

L

M

N

P

R

S

About FranklinCovey

Mission Statement

We enable greatness in people and organizations everywhere.

FranklinCovey (NYSE: FC) is the global consulting and training leader in the areas of strategy execution, customer loyalty, trust, leadership, and individual effectiveness. Clients include 90 percent of the Fortune 100, more than 75 percent of the Fortune 500, thousands of small and midsized businesses, and numerous government entities and educational institutions. FranklinCovey has 46 direct and licensee offices providing professional services in 147 countries. For more information, please visit www.franklincovey.com/tc.

About the Authors

Dr. Stephen R. Covey is an internationally respected leadership authority, teacher, author, organizational consultant, and cofounder and vice chairman of Franklin-Covey Co. He is author of *The 7 Habits of Highly Effective People*, which *Chief Executive* magazine has called the most influential business book of the last 100 years. The book has sold nearly 20 million copies, and after 20 years, still holds a place on most best-seller lists.

Dr. Covey earned an MBA from Harvard and a doctorate from BYU, where he was a professor of organizational behavior. For more than 40 years, he has taught millions of people—including presidents of nations and corporations—the transforming power of the principles that govern individual and organizational effectiveness. He and his wife live in the Rocky Mountains of Utah.

Bob Whitman is chairman of the board and CEO of FranklinCovey.

A Harvard MBA, Whitman was one of four managing partners, CFO, and a board member of Trammell Crow Group. Later, as president and co-CEO of the private equity firm Hampstead Group, he acquired significant equity in and helped a number of companies in the hospitality, retirement housing, restaurant, and theme park industries achieve significant growth. He has served on the board of Wyndham Hotels and Resorts, and as chairman and CEO of Forum Group Inc., now part of Marriott International.

Fascinated by FranklinCovey's mission to help build great and enduring organizations, and already serving on the board, Whitman joined the company as chairman and CEO in January 2000. Since then, he has immersed himself in the inner workings of hundreds of FranklinCovey client organizations to understand what it takes to produce the outcomes of greatness.

An avid mountaineer, rock and ice climber, Whitman enjoys climbing in the Rocky Mountains and the Alps. He has finished the Hawaii Ironman World Triathlon Championship race nine times.

Bob and his wife are the parents of two children and make their home in Salt Lake City, Utah.

Breck England calls himself an "intellectual property architect" who helps create world-class effectiveness solutions for FranklinCovey clients. In his two decades of consulting experience, he has helped some of the world's largest corporations become more effective in their leadership and communication processes. He has directed projects for the Fortune 50 and from Switzerland to Saudi Arabia.

Before joining FranklinCovey, Dr. England served as vice-president of intellectual property for Franklin Quest and director of consulting for Shipley Associates, an international communication-training firm. A PhD in communication, he taught organizational leadership and strategy for seven years in the Marriott School of Management at BYU. He and his wife live on a mountainside in northern Utah.